THE TFX DECISION
McNamara and the Military

Written Under the Auspices of
The Center for International Affairs
Harvard University

THE TFX DECISION

McNamara and the Military

ROBERT J. ART
Brandeis University

LITTLE, BROWN AND COMPANY Boston

*The photographs on pages 14, 28, 52, 84, 110, and 156 are re-
produced with the kind permission of the General Dynamics Corporation of Fort Worth, Texas.*

To my mother and father

PREFACE

The TFX airplane, from the moment it was conceived, has been a subject of controversy within the Department of Defense. It has been so for two reasons. First, the controversy involved issues other than merely performance characteristics and design configurations of an aircraft. It extended to larger, more significant issues: strategic doctrine, service roles, and control over weapon system development. Second, the controversy over this airplane produced a split between the top military officers and their supporting staffs, on the one hand, and the top civilian officials of the Defense Department and their supporting staffs, on the other. In these two respects the TFX controversy is not unique. Many other weapon system disputes of the past, particularly those of the post-World War II era, have centered on such issues and have created such splits within the Defense Department. One such case was the "revolt of the Admirals" in 1949 over the cancellation of a program to build supercarriers that would be capable of launching the B-36 bomber.

Although the TFX controversy is not unique, it is nevertheless a classic case. It is one of the rare instances in which a secretary of Defense retained the support of the secretaries of the services that were adversely affected by the decisions he had made. In the supercarriers decision, Secretary of Defense Louis Johnson had to overrule and then accept the resignation of his secretary of the Navy. In the TFX decision, Secretary of Defense Robert McNamara not only retained the loyalty of his secretaries of the Navy and of the Air Force, but also utilized them to carry through decisions that were highly unpopular in both these services. McNamara was able to achieve, preserve, and utilize a unanimity of viewpoint among the highest civilian officials of the Defense Department. This was something that had seldom, if ever, been done there. The TFX controversy is, then, a classic case of civilian-military relations because the issue of civilian control over the military is so starkly presented. All the people at the pinnacles of civilian authority were unanimous in their views. The top military leaders were similarly united. In their analyses and judgments, each of these united groups was directly opposed to the other. A united military elite thus confronted a united civilian elite.

As well as being a classic case of civilian-military relations, the TFX controversy is one of the few examples of the "McNamara revolution" that is available in detail to the public. By studying the TFX controversy, we can see in microcosm two aspects of this revolution: the novelty of the decisions that McNamara made and the effectiveness of the methods that he used to make them and get them enforced. Because the decisions he made were so novel to the Defense Department, McNamara completely upset traditional expectations and long established bureaucratic habits. Because the methods that he used to make and enforce decisions were so effective, McNamara directly challenged the raison d'être of both the military officers and their supporting staffs. In his actions during the TFX controversy, we can see McNamara signaling to the Defense Department that he was going to run that institution in a style unlike that of any of his predecessors. The TFX controversy is, in effect, a chronicle of how the civilians in the Pentagon gained operating control over the military.

In order to treat the TFX controversy as a study in civilian-military relations, I have done two things. First, I have limited the scope of the book. The following pages deal only with events of the TFX controversy from 1959 through November of 1962. The events occurring after 1962 are qualitatively different from those occurring before. The issues from 1959 through 1962 were political because they centered on who had the authority and power to determine what kind of aircraft would be built and who would build it. By November of 1962, these issues were settled. The issues from 1963 to the present are technical because they have centered on the management of a continuing development program. The major issues of this period have been these: Have development costs been excessive? Has the aircraft met the original performance goals? How useful has the plane been to each service? And how successful has the biservice approach been for weapon system development?

If the issues of the later period are technical, it does not follow that they are less important. In fact it is only by attempting to answer such questions that any judgment about the wisdom of McNamara's two basic decisions on the TFX program — the biservice decision of September, 1961, and the source selection decision of November, 1962 — can be made. I have not tried to answer such questions. Rather than asking whether subsequent events have proven McNamara's two basic decisions to be wise, I have tried to answer a different set of questions. What was each group — the civilians and the military — trying to achieve with the TFX? Can their institutional roles and responsibilities shed any light on why they adopted the goals they did? Did their disputes over the details of aeronautical engineering reflect deeper, underlying perspectives? My approach, in short, has been analytic rather than critical. In treating the TFX controversy, I have therefore presented what the civilian and military leaders thought, how they acted, and, from their own testimony, why they thought and acted as they did.

ROBERT J. ART

ACKNOWLEDGMENTS

I owe a debt of gratitude to many people for the help I received in writing this book. Some unfortunately must remain anonymous. So to those hard-pressed people in government and the aerospace industry I must say a collective "thank you" for the time you freely gave and the patience you always showed. Of those whom I can name, I would like to thank the following: Dan L. Dudas, J. Ronald Fox, Alton Frye, Morton H. Halperin, Robert L. Jervis, William W. Kaufmann, and Kenneth N. Waltz, for your invaluable comments on the manuscript; Morton Halperin and Richard E. Neustadt, for the faith you had in me; Warner R. Schilling, for showing me the way a long time ago; John S. Glaser, Mignon Swihart Gregg, and Doris H. Kearns, for your patient ears and warm hearts; Frederica Kaven, for your complete understanding and unfailing support; David W. Lynch, Luise Mallinger, and Mrs. Gertrude Strelsky, for your help in preparing the manuscript for publication; and Thomas C. Schelling, for inviting me to spend a year at The Center for International Affairs, Harvard University, in order to complete the manuscript.

CONTENTS

Contents

ILLUSTRATIONS AND TABLES

THE TFX DECISION
McNamara and the Military

INTRODUCTION

On November 21, 1962, the Department of Defense announced that a $439 million contract had been awarded to the General Dynamics Corporation to develop a new tactical fighter aircraft. The plane, called the TFX (tactical fighter, experimental) and later named the F-111, incorporated a number of "firsts." It was the first basically new weapon system to be initiated by Robert S. McNamara since he had become secretary of Defense in 1961. It was the first aircraft that had been designed from the start to be used by two military services. It was the first production aircraft to use a variable-sweep wing; the first production aircraft to employ an afterburning turbofan engine; the first tactical fighter designed for trans-Atlantic, nonstop, nonrefueled flight; and the first plane that had combined performance for low altitude, supersonic interdiction with that for high-altitude, subsonic fleet air superiority.

An airplane incorporating so many technological "firsts" would naturally arouse controversy. For in dealing with such large advances in the state of the art, the experts found themselves in disagreement; they were in the realm of uncertainty where assumptions had as much validity as fact — often where only assumptions could be offered because of a dearth of fact. But the uncertainties involved and the large advances in technology sought for are not in themselves sufficient to explain another "first" for the TFX: this was the first instance in which McNamara encountered sustained opposition from Congress to his judgment. An incredible amount of political uproar followed the awarding of this contract. The TFX made the front page of *The New York Times* on and off for almost six months. A certain amount of political "noise" must be expected from congressmen and senators following the awarding of a procurement contract. Political lobbying for contracts is one of the prices we pay for geographic representation. But why in the TFX case were such vituperative, personal charges and countercharges exchanged back and forth between the Senate Permanent Investigating Subcommittee (the McClellan Subcommittee) and the Department of Defense? Why did the hearings of this subcommittee on the awarding of the contract last almost ten months, when most members expected them to be over in four or five days? Why did congressional suspicion, distrust, and disbelief in the motives of Defense Department civilians on the one hand, and Defense Department claims of congressional irresponsibility, meddling, and bias on the other, reach such a frenzied pitch?

The answers to these questions, the reasons for this political uproar, must be sought in areas other than the technological firsts and the normal congressional lobbying for local interests. Another fact about the TFX helps to answer these questions: this program appeared to those in the aerospace industry to be one of the last large military aircraft contracts that would be awarded for the remainder of the 1960's and possibly well into the 1970's. In fact at the time, the TFX appeared to be potentially the largest procurement contract for *one* aircraft program ever to be let by the Defense Department. For, although the development contract amounted to only $439 million, the total contract, including both development and production, would amount to between six and seven billion dollars and maybe more. Where such large sums of money are spent in an industry in which many firms rely heavily upon the government for their existence, competition for these contracts is keen. Where a contract awarded to one of these firms means that it can keep abreast of the rapidly changing technology at government expense and consequently be technically qualified for future contracts, the contract is vital. And where the airframe industry has entered a period when military aircraft contracts are few and far between, for some of these firms these contracts have become matters of sheer survival. The company that received the TFX development contract could thus be reasonably assured of two things: (1) a follow-on production contract for 1,700 to 2,000 planes, an extremely large production run by post-World War II standards; and (2) the place as the leading American producer of tactical fighter aircraft for nearly a decade.

In such an atmosphere, where hungry companies were chasing after a "fat" contract, it would not be unnatural both for political pressures to be brought to bear upon those charged with making the decision and for these pressures to have in fact influenced the awarding of the contract. The men responsible for making the TFX decision did in fact experience political pressures. The secretary of the Air Force involved in the TFX decision has testified to this. That these pressures, however, did bias the responsible authorities, that these men neglected other factors crucial to the decision, that they took the road of political expediency or personal gain, cannot be proved from the evidence available to the public. The problem, however, is much more excruciating: it is not possible to conclude either that political pressures influenced the awarding of the contract or that they did not. In short, the charge of political or personal bias is unanswerable.

Nevertheless, for ten long months in 1963, the senators of the McClellan Subcommittee insisted that the men who made the

TFX contract decision were biased by political pressures and personal interests.* They made these charges directly to these men when they appeared as witnesses before the subcommittee. These men were Fred Korth, secretary of the Navy; Eugene Zuckert, secretary of the Air Force; Roswell Gilpatric, deputy secretary of Defense; and Robert McNamara, secretary of Defense. These senators pointed out that General Dynamics, the winner of the contract, planned to use its Fort Worth, Texas plant to develop the TFX. They then pointed out that Korth was a resident of Fort Worth and a past president of the Continental Bank there. They revealed that this bank had loaned money to General Dynamics and that Korth had kept an active, though not a financial, interest in the activities of this bank. They indicated that Gilpatric, as a past member of the New York law firm of Cravath, Swaine, and Moore, had served as legal counsel to General Dynamics. They charged that Zuckert was somehow politically or personally influenced in his decision because he was born in New York, the state where the principal subcontractor for the TFX contract, the Grumman Company was located.† The charge of political in-

---

* The members of the McClellan Subcommittee were: John L. McClellan, Chairman, Arkansas; Henry M. Jackson, Washington; Sam J. Ervin, North Carolina; Edmund S. Muskie, Maine; Thomas J. McIntyre, New Hampshire; Daniel B. Brewster, Maryland; Karl E. Mundt, South Dakota; Carl T. Curtis, Nebraska; and Jacob K. Javits, New York.

Senators Brewster, McIntyre, and Ervin did not attend the committee hearings on the TFX. Senators Javits and Muskie were generally pro-Administration and hence refrained from such charges. Senator Jackson, because he was from the state where Boeing had its central office and because he was popularly known as "the man from Boeing," tried to remain as neutral as possible. The task of making political hay out of the TFX was left to McClellan, Mundt, and Curtis. They rose to the task. (Hereafter, all bibliographic footnotes are numbered and will be found on pp. 167–175; each explanatory footnote is identified by a symbol and will be found at the bottom of the page.)

† The Grumman Company had its plant on Long Island. It had teamed up with the General Dynamics Corporation with the understanding that it would receive approximately 30 per cent of the work (by dollars) of the contract. It was thus the largest subcontractor to the General Dynamics Corporation.

4

fluence was even thrown point blank at McNamara by Senator Ervin. He said:

> I would like to ask you whether or not there was any connection whatever between your selection of General Dynamics, and the fact that the Vice President of the United States happens to be a resident of the state in which that company has one of its principal if not its principal office?[1]

For ten long months the subcommittee members tried to make the judgments of these men look like cover-ups for personal interest and political expediency. But all that they succeeded in obtaining were flat denials from these men. They gained no real proof. Secretary McNamara's reply to Senator Ervin was, "absolutely none." Zuckert pointed out to Senator Mundt that he had not resided in New York for the past fifteen years, but had been a resident of Maryland. Gilpatric pointed out that he had also done legal work for the Boeing Company, that in fact he had had contacts as a lawyer with many of the largest airframe companies. Finally, Korth stated that because of his peculiar position, he had deliberately refrained from taking a directing hand in this decision (within the Navy) until the last possible moment; that the money that the Continental Bank loaned to General Dynamics was a very small part of a very large loan put together by many banks; and that he was an "American first," "Secretary of the Navy second," and a "resident of Fort Worth, Texas, last."

The unprecedented size of the TFX contract was partly responsible for bringing it into the political limelight, but the senators investigating it were unable to find any concrete proof of conflicts of interest or political deals. Why, then, did these senators claim with such dogged persistence that there had been such conflicts or deals? The answer to this question lies in still another "first" for the TFX and goes a long way to explain its real significance. The TFX represented the first instance in the history of the selection of an advanced weapon system (at least in the experience of those involved) in which the unanimous opinion of the highest

5

military officers of the nation had been overruled by the civilian secretary of Defense.* The two military chiefs — General Le May, Air Force chief of staff, and Admiral Anderson, chief of Naval Operations — and an entire group of top military personnel were unanimous in their opinion: they all recommended awarding the TFX development contract to the Boeing Company.† On the other hand, McNamara and his advisers — Korth, Zuckert, and Gilpatric — unanimously favored General Dynamics. The reason for the senators' insistence thus lay in the fact that the unanimous opinion of military experts had been overruled by four equally unanimous civilians. If both of these sets of leaders, especially the military, had been divided among themselves, then the subcommittee's charges of political influence might have appeared less credible.

Since the subcommittee senators could not prove that the civilian secretaries were politically and personally biased, why did they not try to prove that they were technically wrong? That is, since they could not prove that political influence was used to obtain the contract for General Dynamics, why did they not try to prove that Boeing's proposals were technologically superior at equal cost? In this way they would have achieved the same result:

* This "first" refers only to those decisions made under the System Source Selection Procedure, which will be discussed in Chapters Three and Four.

General Le May said that as vice chief of staff and then as Air Force chief of staff, he had participated in 23 separate source selections and in none of these had the decision made through the Source Selection Procedure been changed by the secretary of Defense. See U.S. Senate, Permanent Subcommittee on Investigations of the Committee on Government Operations, *The TFX Contract Investigation: Hearings,* 88th Cong., 1st Sess., 1963, Vol. 3, p. 698. (Hereafter referred to as the *TFX Hearings.*)

† The lineup of military personnel for Boeing is impressive. Besides Le May and Anderson, there were ten generals and one admiral who served on the Air Council (to be discussed in Chapter Three); General Walter C. Sweeney of the Air Force Tactical Air Command; General Mark E. Bradley of the Air Force Logistics Command; Lieutenant General Bernard Schriever of the Air Force Systems Command; Admiral William E. Ellis, assistant chief of Naval Operations for Air; Rear Admiral Kleber S. Masterson, Bureau of Naval Weapons; and the five generals and flag officers of the Source Selection Board.

to show that the military's decision was unjustly changed. In fact the subcommittee did try this approach. They attempted to prove that a correct, objective procurement decision made by the military was overruled by civilians who were wrong in their technical judgments. This approach, however, suffered from the same difficulty as the first one: it could not be proved. It was impossible for them to conclude who was right and who was wrong, whether Boeing or General Dynamics offered the better plane, simply because the criteria of right and wrong have no meaning when applied to cases like the TFX. This is so for two reasons. First, only one plane was built — that proposed by General Dynamics. There is therefore no chance of ever comparing the performance of the two planes. No positive evidence will ever prove which plane was aerodynamically superior. Second, the only other alternative open to the subcommittee was to do what the military chiefs and civilian secretaries did, namely, to compare "paper airplanes," planes that exist only as designs on the drawing boards and not as concrete objects in the sky. But this method also offers no conclusive answers of right or wrong or of technological superiority. For the areas of unknown and the elements of uncertainty are so great when dealing with "paper airplanes" that even the judgments of experts differ radically, and they did so in the TFX case.

But here we are, faced with probably the largest aircraft procurement contract ever let up to this time by the Defense Department. We have asserted that the political furor arose in part because of the hugeness of the contract, but mainly because the unanimous opinion of the two military services was overruled. And yet we are unable to explain why this decision was overruled. We are unable to conclude either (1) that the military officers were correct in their judgments of the technical factors involved and the civilian secretaries incorrect in theirs; or (2) that the military officers were wrong in their technical judgments and the civilian secretaries right; or (3) that the military officers were right — that Boeing offered the superior proposal — but that the secretaries made their decisions on "political" and not "technical" grounds.

We are unable to explain why this decision was overruled because we, like the senators of the McClellan Subcommittee, have been asking the wrong questions. It is therefore our purpose to ask different kinds of questions in order to explain this decision. Instead of asking who was right and who wrong, or whether political deals were made — both of which are unanswerable — we must rather ask: Why did these two groups of decision makers have different opinions? Were their perspectives the same? What types of factors did each group take into consideration in making their decisions? Were these factors the same? If not, how did they differ? If so, was each given the same value or was it weighted differently by each group? And finally, is there anything inherent in the process used for selecting advanced weapon systems that can help account for these differing, unanimous opinions?

It is our contention that the perspectives of each group of decision makers were indeed different, that each took different factors into account and weighted the same ones differently, and that the process used for selecting advanced weapon systems was peculiarly responsible in one way or another for all these differences. We shall therefore attempt to show that each group of decision makers — the civilian and the military — possessed different criteria for making decisions because their institutional responsibilities, perspectives, and purposes were different. Moreover, we shall attempt to show that the perspectives and purposes of one of these groups, the civilians, had changed from what they had traditionally been and that the other group, the military, either could not or did not comprehend this change or, if they did, refused to take it into account. We attempt to describe, in essence, McNamara's revolutionary changes in the rules of the game — the rules are the criteria for evaluating potential alternatives among weapon systems; the game, the process of deciding which ones to procure.

Thus our purpose is to do these two things: (1) to explain why McNamara made his decision the way he did in the TFX case, that is, why he chose the General Dynamics proposal when the military recommended Boeing's; and (2) to explain why he was able to make and enforce such a decision when the military had traditionally been the final authority for selecting sources to develop their new weapon systems. In short, what were the causes that brought about this decision and what were the methods by which it was made and carried out?

In order to answer these two questions, we must first look at the three years preceding the November, 1962 decision. This is necessary because this decision was preceded by a series of other decisions that vitally affected the evolution of the TFX. In the first part of this book, the first three chapters, we will therefore trace the evolution of the TFX from its origin in 1959 to the awarding of the development contract in November, 1962. In the second part, we will analyze the November decision in light of two special problems connected with procuring advanced weapon systems. In Chapter Four we will discuss, first, the reasons for cost optimism in bids submitted by companies competing for the award of a military contract and second, the difficulties associated with the method used by the Air Force for selecting advanced weapon systems like the TFX. With these two problems in mind, in Chapter Five we will analyze the specific criteria by which the civilian secretaries and military officers evaluated the two proposals submitted by Boeing and General Dynamics. Finally, in Chapter Six, we will touch upon those methods which McNamara devised in order to make and carry out his decision to select the General Dynamics Corporation for developing the TFX.

PART I · THE NARRATIVE

.

The evolution of the TFX airplane, from the moment it was conceived in the daring dreams of a general until the final, tradition-shattering award of the development contract, stretched over four years and two presidential administrations. This history included four exhausting competitions among the interested airframe companies. It was marked by much tension between a determined secretary of Defense and two equally determined military services. It was punctuated by interservice disagreement, dispute, and jealousy between the Air Force and the Navy. At least twice the TFX as a joint program foundered, on the brink of total collapse. It underwent four revisions, being conceived first as a distinct airplane for use by one service only, then as one airplane designed for all three services, to one airplane for two services, until it reached its final form of two versions of one basic plane for use by two services. It involved the dedicated efforts of more than 250 government personnel, who expended several hundred thousand man-hours in evaluating the proposals of the competing airframe companies. In addition to the expense of this evaluation, the competition for the development contract alone cost the government $6 million in paid study contracts to the companies.

In spite of the diversity and changes in its scope, the history of the TFX program falls into three distinct periods. The first period includes the years 1959 and 1960, the last two of the Eisenhower administration. It was then that the Air Force first conceived of the TFX as the follow-on to its F-105 tactical fighter. And it was during these two years that the TFX existed solely as an Air Force program. The second period starts with the beginning of the Kennedy administration in January of 1961 and continues until the end of that year. During that time McNamara changed the TFX from an Air Force program to a joint Air Force-Navy undertaking. It was then that "commonality" became the goal sought for by McNamara and resisted by the two services. "Commonality" was the shorthand way of expressing McNamara's idea that one weapon system could be designed to serve the needs of two or more military services. Finally, the third period embraces the time from January 24, 1962 to November 21, 1962. Then, the number of companies competing for the development contract was reduced from six, to two, to one. It marked an unprecedentedly lengthy competition between two companies under procedures that had never been used. The first phase thus encompasses the origins of the TFX; the second, the introduction and enforced acceptance of the goal of commonality; and the third, the run-off competition between two giants of the airframe industry.

The A (or Air Force) version of the F-111, with wings fully extended.

ONE · THE FIRST PHASE: ORIGINS, 1959–1960

The farsighted general was a man named F. F. Everest; his daring dream, a fighter that could perform in ways never before possible; the time, early in the year 1959. General Everest had just assumed his new post as commander of the Tactical Air Command (TAC) of the Air Force. As commander it was his job to see that TAC could perform its three basic missions dependably and effectively. These were: (1) to obtain and maintain air superiority in the battlefield; this required air-to-air combat; (2) to disrupt the enemy's forces by interdicting his supply caches and supply routes; this involved bombing and/or strafing behind the battlefield area his troops, supplies, aircraft, and anything else militarily useful that could be moved forward to the front lines; and (3) to provide close support for the Army's ground forces; this involved air-to-ground combat.[1] For the first mission, the speed and altitude ceiling of the aircraft were the two most important characteristics; for the second, its range, bomb-load capacity, and penetration speed into hostile territory; for the third, its ability to carry a wide range of weapons (its payload) and to remain in the air for a long time (its "loiter capability").*

The best that the Air Force had to offer in 1959 to perform these three missions was the Republic F-105 fighter. Everest, however, believed that the best was not good enough to cope with the dangers he foresaw looming for TAC in the 1960's. The two most serious of these dangers he judged to be the scarcity of usable overseas airfields and the vulnerability of TAC's aircraft on them. In 1959 TAC had access to 94 of these overseas bases.

---

* These three missions represented TAC's dogma, to which Everest had to pay lip service. It appears, however, that he was interested primarily in having his new aircraft penetrate enemy defenses at a low level at supersonic speeds while carrying nuclear weapons. The reason Everest wanted such an aircraft is self-evident. In the late 1950's American military doctrine still concentrated primarily on maintaining a strategic nuclear retaliatory capability in order to ensure that deterrence was a credible posture. Under such a doctrine, TAC, as well as the Army, suffered from a relative lack of funds. The Air Force received a large share of the military budget; but within that service, the Strategic Air Command (SAC) received the preponderant portion of those funds. By trying to acquire a nuclear capability for TAC and by thus providing it with an ability to deliver nuclear weapons in a way that SAC's B-52 bombers could not (by low level, supersonic interdiction), Everest attempted to protect the present identity of and future role for TAC. (The Army did exactly the same thing when it stressed that the United States lacked an ability to fight limited conventional wars. It too used doctrinal arguments as a means of protecting its service identity and share of defense funds.)

Everest thus saw the TFX as a junior SAC nuclear bomber that would belong to TAC. For this reason the following arguments that he put forth to justify the need for having an aircraft capable of operating from secret, semiprepared airfields were in part merely attempts to rationalize TAC's need for the TFX along lines that suited TAC's then current functions and dogma. For example, the argument that the TFX could operate from semiprepared airfields that would be less vulnerable because they would be more secret ignored the obvious fact that sophisticated equipment and highly trained personnel would be needed on those airfields to service a multimillion dollar aircraft. The Soviets might find it harder to spot semiprepared than concrete airfields, but they could still see the equipment that was there to service the TFX.

With such facts in mind, some of the following arguments advanced by Everest in order to acquire the TFX assume an unreal quality. (This information is based on interviews that I had with those familiar with the early years of the TFX program.)

Eleven were in Europe and of good quality. Of the remaining 83, distributed over the rest of the globe, 33 were of middling quality but nonetheless usable; the other 50 were emergency fields that were either too rough or too short and as a result were totally useless to TAC because the F-105 could not land or take off from them.[2] Of the 94 overseas airfields, then, only 44 were usable. These, however, were immovable, unconcealable targets. They were completely vulnerable to an enemy missile attack, because the Soviets had long ago pinpointed these fields on their military maps.

To increase TAC's flexibility, Everest needed a larger number of usable overseas airfields. To reduce TAC's vulnerability, he needed a larger number of secret overseas airfields. Overseas airfields that were usable, however, were not secret. For the type of fields from which the F-105 could operate required such elaborate preparations that these fields could not be kept hidden from Soviet espionage activities of either the human or nonhuman type. Secrecy and usability, though, were incompatible only because of the limited capabilities of the F-105: airfields with concrete runways up to two miles long were difficult to keep concealed. However, if Everest had a plane that could land and take off from rough, makeshift, dirt airfields, he could use almost any long, reasonably flat area. The flexibility in choosing airfields that such a plane would produce would give him the secrecy he wanted. Or if he had a plane that could fly nonstop over both oceans, it could be based in the United States. Then he would have to worry less about either the suitability or the secrecy of his overseas bases.

Everest demanded a new plane having both these characteristics. He wanted a craft that could land and take off, not from concrete runways, but from sod fields whose length would be half that required by the F-105. He also asked for a plane that could travel nonstop and without refueling over the Atlantic Ocean. Yet even a plane with these unheard-of capabilities did not satisfy Everest. For, merely to reduce the vulnerability of the planes on

TAC's overseas bases by increasing the number that were secret and usable would serve no useful military purpose, unless these planes at the same time embodied the furthest possible advances in aircraft technology. In this way the plane probably could cope with anything that the enemy might put in the air against it. Everest therefore required from this new plane that it travel extremely long distances, carry a load of nuclear weapons, and fly at tree-top levels (called "on the deck") in order to escape early radar detection.* Then it could perform its interdiction mission. He insisted that it engage in aerial combat at high altitudes and at speeds in excess of 1,700 miles per hour. Then it could perform its air-superiority mission. Finally, he stipulated that this plane have a large ordnance-carrying capacity. Then it could perform its ground-support mission.[3]

A plane with these characteristics would reduce TAC's overseas vulnerability, increase its operational flexibility, and perform the required missions with superior performance. A plane with these characteristics, however, had never been designed or built because it had been technologically impossible to do so. The physical problems encountered had not yet been solved. The principal difficulty lay with the wings. Everest wanted a plane that could fly on the deck at supersonic speeds and that could also span the Atlantic Ocean without stopping or refueling. The first was called the "dash" mission; the second, the "ferry" mission. Aerodynamically, these were conflicting missions.[4] On the one hand, if the plane were to fly at supersonic speeds on the deck, then it would need both a short wingspan (the distance from wing tip to wing tip) and a high angle of sweep (the angle by which the wings depart from a straight line as they are swept back, that is, as they become V-shaped).† On the other hand, if the plane were to fly

---

* Radar can see only in a straight line. For example, at a 50-foot altitude, radar can see only 60 to 80 miles to the horizon. Therefore, the lower a plane approaches its target, the longer it will take before radar can detect it.

† Of course, the wingspan depends partly on the angle of sweep. If the length of each wing remains the same, the smaller the angle of sweep (the

such long distances, then it would need exactly the reverse: a long wingspan and a low angle of wing sweep.*

For the dash mission, the greater the speed, the more friction and drag the plane would generate. Because of the higher density of the atmosphere at very low altitudes, increases in speed would produce proportionately more drag than they would at higher altitudes. For supersonic speeds on the deck, almost any wing would therefore be too much for the aircraft because it would increase the surface area of the plane.† The larger the surface area of the plane, the more air friction would be produced. With large, low-swept wings, gusts and turbulent air would cause the plane to be buffeted severely when flying at supersonic speeds at such low altitudes.** Thus for the low-level dash mission Everest's plane would require the delta configuration: short, small wings swept back very far.

For the ferry mission, however, the extremely long distances to be traveled would require that the plane fly at low speeds, at high altitudes, and with wings of a long span.[5] The principal factor here, as with the dash mission, would be the amount of drag generated. In this case, however, the purpose would be to reduce the drag in order to conserve fuel. The plane would consume proportionately less fuel for the same distance traveled if it flew at subsonic rather than supersonic speeds. Subsonic speeds require less

---

more the wings are swept back), the smaller the wingspan becomes. But with a given angle of sweep, the wingspan can be increased by increasing the length of each wing.

* Ideally, the wings would have a zero degree sweep; that is, they would form a straight line.

† Technically, more important than the surface area is the cross-sectional area distribution, because it is the primary factor in producing wave drag at supersonic speeds. Highly swept wings provide less maximum cross-sectional area, as well as a better distribution of area (slopes). (I am indebted to Dan L. Dudas of the General Dynamics Corporation, Fort Worth, Texas, for this technical note.)

** At tree-top levels a plane with a long wingspan and large wing area could subject the pilot to as much as three G's of buffeting.

energy (fuel) than supersonic speeds. It would consume proportionately less fuel for the same distance traveled if it flew at high rather than low altitudes. High altitudes produce less air friction than low altitudes because of lower atmospheric density. Finally, it would consume proportionately less fuel for the same distance traveled if it had a long wingspan and a large wing area rather than a short span and small area. A long wingspan and large wing area yield more lift with less attendant drag and hence require less energy (fuel) to propel the plane through the air than a short span and small area. For the ferry mission Everest's plane would thus require the more traditional configuration: long, large wings swept back very little. Figure 1.1 illustrates the wing configuration for the dash and ferry missions.

If Everest's plane were to perform the supersonic low-level dash mission and the subsonic high-altitude ferry mission, it would be the first such multimission aircraft. If his plane were to perform both these missions, however, it would have to have wings that could be moved from the position required for supersonic flight to that required for subsonic flight. In other words, it would have to possess wings whose angle of sweep could be changed. This idea — to vary the angle of sweep — was not new. Two companies had experimented with the variable-sweep wing early in the 1950's. The Bell Aircraft Company had built the X-5; the Grumman Company, the F-10-F.[6] Both planes were impractical as operational aircraft, but each demonstrated the feasibility of the variable-sweep wing. Each, however, had suffered from the same fundamental difficulty: to change the angle of sweep, it was necessary to move the entire wing structure fore and aft, because the pivot point for the wing had been placed inside the fuselage at the wing root.[7] As a result of this design, the sweeping of the entire wing had upset the longitudinal stability of these planes by moving their centers of gravity and centers of lift. The point where the centers of gravity and lift lay differed with each angle of sweep. These two centers, however, had to coincide if the aircraft was to

20

FIGURE 1.1   *The Variable-Sweep Wing*

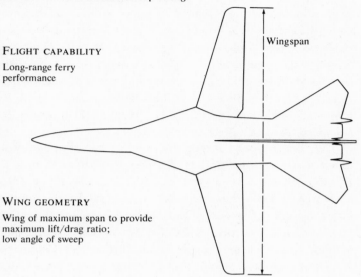

FLIGHT CAPABILITY

Long-range ferry
performance

WING GEOMETRY

Wing of maximum span to provide
maximum lift/drag ratio;
low angle of sweep

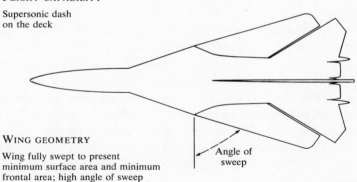

FLIGHT CAPABILITY

Supersonic dash
on the deck

WING GEOMETRY

Wing fully swept to present
minimum surface area and minimum
frontal area; high angle of sweep

21

remain stable in flight. The result was thus the same: each of these planes was unstable in flight. It was not until 1960 that variable-sweep-wing-fuselage combinations were so designed that the wings could be moved while the balanced center of gravity and center of lift were still maintained. This breakthrough was accomplished by placing the pivot point on the wing and hence outside of the fuselage. In this way only a part of the wing would move, with the rest remaining stationary, permanently.[8] Figure 1.2 illustrates the positions of these two types of pivot points.

The man primarily responsible for this breakthrough was John Stack, assistant director of the Langley Research Center, a facility of the National Aeronautics and Space Administration (NASA). In March of 1960, Stack reported to General Everest that he had tested his new wing design and believed it technically sound. By late April a conference of the Air Force Air Research and Development Command, the Air Force Tactical Air Command, and NASA had produced joint agreement on a program for developing a tactical fighter that would use this new variable-sweep design. The plane, the TFX, would require a program costing more than $2.2 billion. Sixteen test aircraft would be produced for $338 million. The first test flight would come in May of 1963; operational availability, by October of 1965.[9]

The TAC sent a request to Air Force Headquarters, asking that it be allowed to proceed with this program. Headquarters in turn ordered the Air Force Systems Command to prepare a feasibility study on the plane. This study was completed by June. It was favorable. Air Force Headquarters then obtained the verbal consent of the Defense Department's Director of Research and Engineering to proceed with the selection of a contractor to develop the TFX. It thereupon issued a specific operational requirement (SOR). This document (SOR 183) described specifically the operational requirements the TFX would have to meet and the missions it would have to perform.[10] The Aeronautical Systems Division of the Systems Command and TAC spent the rest of the

FIGURE 1.2   *Methods of Sweeping the Wing*

F-10-F and X-5

METHOD OF SWEEP

Wing pivots from point inside fuselage;
entire wing sweeps and translates
for aerodynamic balance

TFX

METHOD OF SWEEP

Wing pivots from point on wing outside
fuselage; only part of wing sweeps

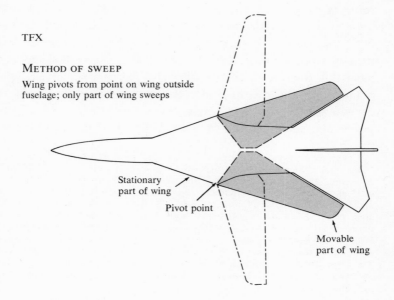

summer and part of the fall drawing up a work statement that would be issued to the aircraft industry in October or November, along with the SOR. The work statement went into much greater detail about the processes, materials, tests, and performance goals involved in developing the TFX.*

While the Air Force had been developing and refining its ideas about this new tactical fighter, two other developments that would affect the fate of the TFX had been taking place. The first involved the aircraft industry; the second, the Navy. One of the keys to the survival of a company in the aircraft business in 1959 (as now) was its ability to predict future military requirements. This predictive ability was so vital because it enabled a company to begin development work on an airplane design long before the military service had formally requested such designs from the industry. This early development work in turn could provide a company with a head start over other firms. If the company had progressed far enough in its work by the time the military services formally made their requests, no other company could possibly hope to close the gap and offer equally good designs, and certainly not better ones. Prediction could therefore bring contracts. Prediction, however, was inherently risky: the chances that the company was working in areas that would interest the services were naturally subject to gross errors; and yet, this work involved great expense for the company in time, money, and scarce skilled manpower that could be used for other projects. If the company had

* This is how the Department of Defense describes a work statement: "The work statement must describe the application which the various areas of science and technology have in the work to be done. It must also reflect total engineering and development requirements, including laboratory work and tests. It must cover tooling concepts. Support equipment needs must be envisioned. Training requirements both personnel and devices must be covered. Testing programs — static testing and flight testing in the case of aircraft and missiles — must be developed. And, above all, the performance goals which the new weapon system is to achieve must be clearly identified." See Department of Defense, *Procurement Presentation to the Procurement Subcommittee of the Committee on Armed Services* (U.S. Senate, Washington, D.C., 1960), p. 29.

guessed wrong, all its costly efforts would be wasted. Nonetheless, the aircraft companies had to predict to survive.

This was exactly what the Boeing Company had been doing since the early months of 1959. It had been betting that the Air Force would soon be interested in procuring a variable-sweep wing fighter for operational use. It had in early 1959 made contact with two persons: with Stack to obtain his designs and with Everest to divine Air Force desires. By that summer it had developed reasonably good designs for a variable-sweep wing airplane.[11] It had kept the military services interested by informing them of its progress by means of numerous brochures. Its development work had included "full-scale mockups, laboratory system tests, extensive wind tunnel tests of various configurations, and numerous structural tests on critical elements of the air vehicle."[12] It was continuing to refine and improve its designs during the summer and fall of 1960. By contrast, the General Dynamics Corporation did not begin work on variable-sweep wing technology until 1960.[13] The Boeing Company had thus built up a year's lead time over General Dynamics.

The second development during this early period involved the Navy. Like the Air Force, it had been thinking about its future aircraft needs. Unlike the Air Force, however, one of these needs — the most important in Navy eyes — would not be served by an aircraft capable of flying behind enemy lines at high speeds and at extremely low altitudes. Rather it would be served by an aircraft capable of circling a fleet of ships at high altitudes for long periods. Equipped with a high-performance air-to-air missile, this plane, which the Navy planned to call the F-6D Missileer as its follow-on to the F-4H tactical fighter, would be able to locate and destroy up to 20 miles away any enemy aircraft approaching the fleet. This mission of "fleet air defense" therefore required two things in a plane: (1) long endurance in the air and (2) a complex missile system.*

---

* The Navy, of course, had other air missions besides fleet defense. One

The first of these requirements, however, precluded the necessity for supersonic performance; the second, the possibility of it. To be able to spot effectively any incoming enemy aircraft, the Missileer would have to circle the fleet (called "loitering on station") for several hours at a distance of about 150 miles. To prolong its time on station, it would have to fly at subsonic speeds. To destroy enemy aircraft at distances of up to 20 miles, the Missileer would need to have in its fuselage nose a panoramic search radar with an antenna whose radius would be about five feet.[14] With an antenna of this size in the nose, the frontal area of the fuselage would be too wide to permit the plane to achieve supersonic flight. The Missileer was thus an airplane built around a huge radar antenna. It was a single-mission aircraft.*

The Air Force had thus been defining its requirements for a high speed, multimission aircraft. It was preparing to issue requests for designs in November. The Navy had obtained tentative approval in the early part of 1960 to proceed with the development of a single-mission aircraft. It was seeking additional funds for development. In spite of their differences in mission and design, both the TFX and the Missileer encountered the same obstacle: a directive from Secretary of Defense Gates to halt further work. The Eisenhower administration was reluctant to commit the Kennedy administration to any major weapon system programs.[15] As a result, this directive prevented the Air Force from issuing its requests to industry for the TFX and the Navy from proceeding with further work on the Missileer and its missile system. Funds

---

of these was ground support for Marine beach landings. Only the fleet air defense mission is considered here, however, because it was the mission that the Navy fought hardest to have the TFX fulfill and that was therefore the most difficult to reconcile with Air Force requirements.

* Opinion in the Navy was sharply divided on whether or not to proceed with the development of the Missileer. Opponents argued that an aircraft capable of only subsonic flight and a single mission could not survive in the 1960's, much less in the 1970's. Proponents argued that these facts were indeed true, but that they were overcome by the proposed high-performance air-to-air missile.

for the development of the Missileer were deleted from the fiscal 1962 defense budget.

By the end of November, 1961, then, the first phase in the evolution of the TFX had come to a close. Because of the forceful prodding of a farsighted officer, the Air Force had developed plans for a new tactical fighter that would require tremendous advances in aeronautical engineering. At least two aircraft companies had been working on designs for such an aircraft. The Air Force had been on the verge of requesting design proposals from the aircraft industry when the secretary of Defense had ordered a halt to all development programs for major new weapon systems. Throughout this period, though the TFX was to be a multimission aircraft, it had remained a single-service program. But what changes, if any, would the new administration bring? Would the Air Force be allowed to proceed on its own with a program to develop a tactical fighter for the 1960's and 1970's? Or would it be forced into channels that it would stubbornly resist? Would the missions of this plane remain the same? Or would they be modified to accommodate those of the Navy? Finally, what effect would this man from Ford have on either the TFX or the Missileer or both? To these questions we now turn.

The F-111A, with wings fully swept for high-speed flight.

TWO · THE SECOND PHASE: COMMONALITY, FEBRUARY– DECEMBER, 1961

The second phase in the TFX program lasted from February to December of 1961. It marked a major reorientation in both the design and mission of this plane. It saw the TFX transformed from a single-service program to a biservice one. It was during the second phase that McNamara began to make his new ideas and approaches felt in the field of weapons procurement. The year 1961 was thus the period of commonality.

Three distinct intervals made up this second phase: (1) the February decision; (2) the period of stalemate, March through August; and (3) the September decision. With the February decision McNamara decided to develop one plane, and one plane only, which would fulfill the tactical fighter needs of all military branches — Air Force, Navy, Marine Corps, and Army. During the stalemate McNamara modified his original intention: he would now develop two aircraft to fill the needs of the four branches. One of these, the TFX, would serve both the Air Force and the Navy. From March through August the Air Force and Navy were struggling, each trying to have its own requirements represented in the joint program to the detriment of those of the other. It was a period without progress because no agreement was reached between the two services. With the September decision, McNamara ended this stalemate by unilaterally setting the limits within which each service could work to satisfy its own needs.

The February Decision

The New Frontier was a period of studied and conscious rethinking of American life. Its style was one of "youthful vigor" and unemotional, "cool" intellectual logic. If John Kennedy set this style for the nation as a whole, then the man whom he selected for his secretary of Defense did the same for that department. As a professor at the Harvard Business School before World War II, a lieutenant colonel in the Army Air Forces during that war, and president of the Ford Motor Company in 1960, Robert S. McNamara had had much varied experience in exercising his "cool" analytical mind. An amazing facility with figures, an incredible memory, and an almost unimaginable grasping for and grasp of details — these were his forte. Possessed of a brilliant mind, a strong will, and a determined dedication to hard work, having the confidence of his president and the consequent freedom to pursue his own way, and convinced that changes were needed, McNamara — whom few people in Washington had heard of before he assumed his post — proceeded to remake the Department of Defense.

He wrought two revolutions in that institution: one in strategic doctrine; the other in the method of making decisions. The first was called the strategy of "flexible response"; the second, the "cost-effectiveness" technique. Each was dependent upon the other. On the one hand, the change in strategy would not be effective unless a method could be found for translating the theoretical doctrine into the actual, desired kinds of power. On the other, the method of making decisions would be useless by itself because it could only point out the best way of achieving the goal that the strategy had to choose. For Kennedy and McNamara this goal was simple and straightforward: to provide the United States with what they both were convinced it lacked, namely, a much wider ranger of options in using its national power. Through the strategy of flexible response, they sought to give to America alternatives for meeting aggression other than those either of resorting to nuclear war or of doing nothing. They wanted to make the force used commensurate with the danger posed. The strategy of flexible response was "flexible" precisely because it offered a choice of responses. And because it was flexible, it was also controllable. Although the United States already possessed the ability to wage nuclear war, either general or limited, strategic or tactical, McNamara believed that these nuclear forces needed to be strengthened by increasing their numbers and reducing their vulnerability to attack. But the area in which he felt America's force was most deficient was in its ability to wage nonnuclear, conventional wars. It was in this area that he began immediate, large-scale efforts.[1]

If the strategy of flexible response represented McNamara's goal of providing choices in the ways in which the United States could reply to aggression, then his method of making decisions, the cost-effectiveness technique, represented his means of achieving this goal. With this technique McNamara attempted to solve military problems by an economic analysis. He borrowed the logic of choice from economic theory and applied it to the military problems of the Defense Department. The logic of choice dictated that each unit of input — human, material, or monetary — must produce the maximum unit of military output, whatever form that unit might take. It aimed at achieving the most efficient use of scarce resources with the minimum waste.[2]

With this technique McNamara demanded that all possible alternative ways of approaching each military problem (that his strategy defined) be costed *before* and not *after* the decision had been made on which alternative to use. In this way cost would not serve as the test of whether a military program was feasible, that is, whether the defense budget would permit it; rather, cost would serve as one of the guides in choosing among the alternatives. Instead of drawing up programs purely on the basis of "military requirements," costing each program, and then determining whether it was feasible to proceed with it within given budgetary constraints, McNamara insisted that costs be considered *when* formulating the programs to meet the military requirements. Then the budget would not predetermine the strategy to be followed; rather the strategy would determine the size of the defense budget. In this way not only could the cost of each alternative be known and compared to the others, but also the most economical way of providing each alternative could be found. McNamara's method would tell him ". . . that the choices that maximize military power with given resources . . . [would be] the same choices that minimize the cost of attaining that level of power."[3] Through the cost-effectiveness technique McNamara could thus relate the military effectiveness of a program (the output) to its cost (the input).*

---

* A concrete example might make this approach clearer. Suppose that one military problem requiring solution is how best to defend Washington, D.C., from a surprise missile attack. With the cost-effectiveness technique, all possible military methods would be listed, for example, bomb shelters, antimissile missiles, airplanes on fifteen minutes' notice equipped with air-to-air missiles, etc. Each approach would then be costed and an estimate would be made of its military usefulness or effectiveness in knocking out incoming missiles. In this way the cost of each alternative solution would be known, as well as the number of missiles it could be expected to destroy. Then the most effective way of destroying the incoming missiles for a given cost could be chosen.

This method of making decisions differs from the "requirements" approach. Here the best way to defend Washington would be chosen on the basis of military judgment from the alternatives listed. The method selected would then be costed to decide whether or not there were enough funds within the budgetary constraints to select this approach. If not, another approach would be estimated to determine its feasibility.

In the first method, alternatives are costed and compared with each other. In the second, they are costed and compared with the budgetary

Both McNamara's strategy of flexible response and his cost-effectiveness technique affected the TFX program. The strategy persuaded him to proceed with the program, but the technique made him alter it drastically. Both effects, however, were brought about by the same feature of the TFX: its multimission capability. Because of his strategic doctrine McNamara wanted options to avoid an all-out nuclear war. He therefore desired flexibility in the ways in which he could use America's force. The TFX appeared to McNamara to offer some of that flexibility. If he wanted to bomb selected enemy homeland targets, he could do so with the TFX. It could carry nuclear weapons and escape radar detection to deliver them. If he wanted to do the same thing with conventional weapons, he could do so with the TFX. If he had to ensure air superiority in a conventional war, he could do so with the TFX. If he had to have information on enemy troop movements, he could obtain it with the TFX. Or if he needed to rush planes to some distant spot with only hours to spare, he could do so with the TFX. The TFX was a bomber, a fighter, a reconnaissance craft, and a transoceanic airplane. It could use nuclear and non-nuclear weapons. It could be used in a strategic or tactical role. Its ability to perform all these missions convinced McNamara that the TFX could help provide him with those choices he demanded.[4]

But why should a plane with all these capabilities be used by only one military branch? If this plane could provide air superiority in order to protect troops on the battlefield, why could it not do so for ships at sea? If it could fly nonstop, without refueling, over the Atlantic, why could it not loiter on station for long

---

funds available. With the cost-effectiveness approach the size of the military program fixes the level of defense expenditures. With the requirements approach the size of the military program is fixed by the predetermined level of defense expenditures.

Of course, the cost-effectiveness technique will not decide whether it is important to defend Washington from a surprise missile attack. It is only a tool. It shows how to do so in the most effective way for a given cost once the decision has been made to do so.

periods around the fleet? If it could provide close ground support for Army troops, why could it not do so for Marines? McNamara reasoned that if the TFX could be designed with so many capabilities just for the Air Force, then these very capabilities could easily meet the needs of all four military branches. That is, the potential effectiveness of the TFX as a weapon system would be most fully realized if it were not confined to Air Force use alone. In the process the costs of new tactical fighters for the services would be minimized, because only one aircraft would have to be developed in order to fulfill the tactical fighter needs of all four branches. McNamara would not have to purchase four separate tactical fighters, conduct four separate development test programs, carry on four separate training programs, purchase four separate stocks of replacement spares, or maintain four separate logistics units.[5] Instead he could take advantage of the economies of scale that only one aircraft program would offer. Through commonality McNamara could thus fully realize the potential military effectiveness of the TFX and at the same time minimize the cost of a new tactical fighter program. He decided to proceed with the development of this multimission aircraft, but on a multiservice basis.

McNamara reached these two decisions after he had received recommendations for a multiservice fighter-bomber program from a special study panel that he had directed to examine the ability of the United States to wage limited war.* Under directions from McNamara, Herbert F. York, Director of Defense Research and Engineering (DDR & E), on February 14 ordered all the services to study the development of a joint experimental tactical fighter, the TFX, basing their studies on the tactical fighter then under consideration by the Air Force. The services were then to prepare a "coordinated specific operational requirement and technical development plan for his [York's] approval."[6]

* This panel was headed by Paul H. Nitze, assistant secretary of Defense for International Security Affairs.

The Period of Stalemate: March–August

Initial Opposition. McNamara had made his decision. Upon his instructions York had then acted. How would the services react? The answer was not long in coming. For on March 9, York received a memorandum on the TFX from Dr. James H. Wakelin, Jr., then assistant secretary of the Navy for Research and Development. In this memorandum Wakelin said:

> As a result of the discussions and evaluations conducted thus far, regarding the TFX (SOR 183) aircraft, the Navy considers that the TFX is not suitable for Navy use since it has little or no application to meet Navy or Marine missions. The Navy now has better aircraft for our purposes in being and development.[7]

After expressing the Navy's general opposition, Wakelin went into more detail. He said that the McDonnell F-4H, the Navy's newest and best tactical aircraft, and the Missileer then under consideration, were and would be far better than the TFX for the Navy's superiority mission. He pointed out that the F-4H, already available, had better radar, better missiles, and better tactical air control than that proposed for the TFX. He expressed strong reservations about the compatibility of the TFX with the Navy's aircraft carriers.* He summarized the Navy's evaluation of the TFX as a "large, complex, expensive aircraft basically unsuited for limited war missions" but useful for nuclear attacks.†

The Navy also reacted swiftly to McNamara's "new experiment in living" — commonality. "Peaceful coexistence" was not for the Navy. It would rather fight than switch — fight to develop its own tactical fighter than switch to that based on the designs of another service. Wakelin ended his memorandum with a highly critical opinion of commonality:

> I am concerned about what appears to be overemphasis on a single aircraft configuration to meet these vital operational na-

---

* All these points will be discussed in much more detail.

† This was precisely the type of TFX General Everest had envisioned. See Chapter One, p. 16.

tional defense requirements. The technical and operational risks of such a single course of action are not, in my view, consistent with national defense interests.[8]

As the official spokesman for the Navy and Marines and as the unofficial one for the Army, Wakelin's formal recommendation was: "drop the TFX altogether." But informally he requested that York set up a committee of representatives from all the services that would review their combined tactical air requirements. Since he had received nothing but opposition to his February 14 directive, York agreed. He made Wakelin a member of this committee, the Committee on Tactical Air, and appointed Fred Wolcott of DDR & E its chairman.[9]

The Committee on Tactical Air. York apparently thought not only that the concept of a joint TFX program required further study, but also that the best way to achieve a consensus on this program lay in such a committee. He also believed that two other subjects needed further study: (1) the Navy Missileer project; and (2) the close-support requirements of the Army and Marine Corps. Since the TFX might very well cause the Missileer to be canceled and since it might be the plane to perform all future close-support missions, he included these two subjects on the committee's agenda. During March, April, and May, the Committee on Tactical Air thus reviewed the entire spectrum of tactical air requirements for the 1962–1971 time frame. It examined what kinds of aircraft would be required to provide continental air defense for the North American Air Defense Command, all-weather interdiction for the Tactical Air Command, fleet air defense for the Navy, and close air support for Army and Marine Corps amphibious landings and other combat operations.[10]

After many meetings it became clear to the Committee that one aircraft could not be developed to perform all the missions to the complete satisfaction of every service. The greatest stumbling block apparently lay in the difficulty the committee had in reconciling the close air support mission with the others. For close air support the aircraft would have to carry out offensive and defensive strikes against selected enemy ground targets in the battlefield area. For all-weather interdiction it would have to carry out the same kinds of strikes, except that these would be behind the front lines, deep in enemy territory. For both fleet air defense and continental air defense, the plane would have to engage in air-to-air combat with enemy craft. To perform the last three missions effectively — all-weather interdiction, fleet air defense, and continental air defense — the aircraft would have to be capable of doing the same thing: achieving superiority in the air. It would have to be capable of destroying any and all enemy aircraft that it might encounter. Achieving air superiority was, of course, the basic purpose of the fleet and continental air defense missions. It was not the basic purpose of the all-weather interdiction mission, but it was necessary if the plane were to perform this mission successfully. It had to be able to destroy attacking enemy aircraft if it were to deliver its bombs.

It seems that the same reasoning should apply to the close-support mission: achieving air superiority was necessary if the plane were to provide close support. For the plane could not freely and successfully attack ground targets if it were subject to attack from the air. The Army and Navy, however, did not reason quite in this manner. They wanted the lightest, smallest, most easily operated aircraft possible to provide close support for the ground troops.[11] The reasons they gave were simple: the lighter, smaller, and more easily operated the plane, the lower the cost. And the lower the cost, the more planes would there be available. The Army and Navy did not want to burden the plane with an air superiority capability, for that would increase the complexity, increase the cost, and hence reduce the number available. They wanted a single-mission aircraft for their close-support needs.*

* The Army and Navy apparently did not reason either that another aircraft would be necessary to provide air superiority if they insisted on such a close-support aircraft or that the expense of this other aircraft would

As a result of these deliberations, the Committee on Tactical Air reached the conclusion that two separate development programs would be necessary: one to develop an unsophisticated, inexpensive, close-support aircraft; the other, a complex, high-performance aircraft. The first should be called the VAX (attack aircraft, experimental); the second, the TFX (tactical fighter, experimental). The VAX should perform the close-support mission for ground combat operations; the TFX, the interdiction, fleet air defense, and continental air defense missions.* The Navy should administer the VAX development program; the Air Force, the TFX development program.[12] The latter, however, should remain a biservice (Air Force-Navy) venture. Though the Air Force would manage the program, the requirements of both the Air Force and Navy should be ·met by the same plane. The services had thus succeeded in challenging and thwarting Mc-Namara's first decision. He had wanted to develop only one aircraft to fulfill all future tactical fighter missions. The services obtained DDR & E's agreement for two. Shortly the Air Force and Navy would try to increase this number to three.

Air Force vs. Navy Needs. McNamara had made his original decision in February because he had believed then that an aircraft designed to perform many missions for one service could be easily modified to perform many missions for several services. However, both the deliberations and conclusions of the Committee on Tacti-

---

necessarily reduce the number of close-support aircraft they could have. The reasons for their insistence on a single-mission, close-support aircraft thus appear puzzling. But from the evidence, it is not possible to explain this apparent puzzle.

* If it were possible, the TFX was also to provide fire support (close support) for Marine Corps amphibious and beachhead landing operations. In the TFX program, the fleet air defense mission became known as Navy Mission A; the fire-support mission, as Navy Mission B. Mission A always remained the primary Navy mission. Mission B came as a by-product of Mission A. That is, if the plane could loiter on station for many hours, it could also fly the long distances to support beachhead operations. (It would have to fly such long distances because it was necessary for the aircraft carriers to remain out of the range of land-based enemy aircraft.)

cal Air and the analysis by his own staff convinced him that the TFX could not be fully effective for the Army and Marine Corps close-support roles. He therefore ratified the conclusions of the Committee on Tactical Air. He then instructed Air Force Secretary Zuckert to make another attempt to obtain the Navy's concurrence in the specifications that the Air Force had drawn up for its follow-on to the F-105. These specifications would serve as the basis for a joint Air Force-Navy TFX development program.[13]

After analyzing the studies done by his staff, McNamara still held the opinion that one aircraft could be designed to meet the performance requirements of both services. He reasoned that this was possible because the primary Navy mission of fleet air defense and the primary Air Force mission of long-range interdiction, though different in their purposes, were nevertheless similar enough in the aerodynamic and operational features that each would require in a plane that one, not two, planes could be built to perform them both. Each mission would need an aircraft capable of achieving air superiority. Both would probably require a plane equipped with air-to-air missiles. Each would need a high-performance radar system. Both would require a plane capable of remaining in the air for many hours — the one for loitering on station; the other for long flights over the ocean or for deep penetration into enemy territory. Each would need an all-weather capability. If the operational characteristics that each mission would require the plane to have were markedly similar, McNamara reasoned that the variable-sweep wing would make it feasible to reduce the need for those characteristics which were dissimilar to a point that was manageable. Because it was now thought feasible to build an operational plane with movable wings, a multimission aircraft was seen as a real possibility.

McNamara considered his reasoning to be sound. The Air Force and, to a greater extent, the Navy, did not. They contended that the performance requirements of their respective missions were so different that to design one aircraft to perform both missions would compromise each of them. Neither service was eager to participate in a joint development program. The Navy, especially, feared that its aircraft needs would be lost in a program managed by the Air Force. The fact that the number of planes it would receive would be only a seventh of the production run reinforced this fear.* Each service wanted to retain the privilege of autonomously developing its own weapon systems and consequently of tailoring them as much as possible to its respective needs. Both considered that it would be unwise to base the entire performance needs of both services for the next generation of tactical aircraft on one development effort.[14] Each could not help but view this joint development program as one further step in the integration or blurring of service lines that had been progressing steadily since the enactment of the National Security Act of 1947.

McNamara thus encountered strong opposition from the military officers of both services to a joint TFX development program. These officers, however, did not express their opposition openly by using language that justified the necessity for maintaining service autonomy. Rather they disguised it by couching it in the technical jargon of aerodynamics. The responsible military officers chose to argue on grounds of technical nonfeasibility instead of expressing their mutual desires of maintaining their respective service identities.†

The Air Force presented its case in the following manner. It wanted the TFX to be designed for the long-range interdiction

* The production run contemplated at this time was to be 1,700 planes, of which 250 would be allotted to the Navy. Later, in 1963, after the contract was let, the Navy decided to double its order to about 500 planes.

† This is my opinion after closely reading the entire transcript of the *TFX Hearings.* An official of the Defense Department, A. W. Blackburn, expresses the same view. He was in the Office of Tactical Weapons, DDR & E. Blackburn was one of the few, perhaps the only, high DOD civilian officials to be intimately associated with the TFX from its inception in 1959 down to the November, 1962 decision. He was the man in DDR & E assigned to keep track of the progress of the TFX.

mission. It summarized the performance requirements for this mission with the phrase "high-low-high." It wanted the TFX to be capable of flying at *high* altitudes for 3,600 miles, to approach the target at *low* altitudes (on the deck) at mach 1.2 for 30 minutes (a distance of 400 miles), and to escape from the target at *high* altitudes (over 30,000 feet).* To fly that far, the plane would have to carry a great deal of fuel. It would therefore have a heavy takeoff weight. To fly that fast that low, it would have to have a heavy frame in order to stand the pressures produced by severe buffeting. This frame would increase the takeoff weight. To fly that fast that low or high, it would also have to have a relatively long, narrow configuration. That would be the best aerodynamic shape for supersonic speeds at any altitude. The Air Force feared that it would have to compromise each of its performance standards if it had to meet those of the Navy.

The Air Force was right. It would have to do so if the Navy persisted in its demands. The Navy had no need for such long ferry ranges. Its aircraft carriers would transport the plane wherever it had to go. The Navy had no need for high-speed performance at low altitudes. The plane would hover around the fleet at low speeds and high altitudes. The Navy had no need to deliver nuclear bombs and then escape at high altitudes and at supersonic speeds over missle-defended territory. The plane would circle the fleet, locate, and then destroy any approaching enemy aircraft with long-range air-to-air missiles. The performance requirements for the Navy's primary mission of fleet air defense therefore suggested an aerodynamic configuration different from that desired by the Air Force. Because the Navy used the charac-

* These figures may not be exact. They vary depending on the magazine consulted. I have no way of knowing the exact figures since all were deleted from the *TFX Hearings* by the Defense Department on the grounds of national security. (The figures above come from W. T. Gunston, "TFX: A Next Generation Military Aeroplane," *Flight International,* LXXXI (February 8, 1962), p. 208; and R. A. Smith, "The 7-Billion Dollar Contract That Changed the Rules," *Fortune,* LXVII (March, 1963), p. 100.)

teristics of the Missileer as its initial bargaining position with the Air Force, it desired a relatively "fat" plane.[15] Since it wanted a long-range radar system, the Navy would need a large antenna in its plane. As with the Missileer, the width of this antenna would mean a fat fuselage nose. But every increase in the frontal area of the plane would increase fuel consumption tremendously.[16] The increase in fuel consumption in turn would reduce both the ferry range the plane could travel and the supersonic speeds it could attain.

Although the Navy's fleet air defense mission put limits on the narrowness of the fuselage, on the range, and on the speed of the aircraft, its need to provide for "carrier compatibility" restricted the length, height, and weight of the aircraft. By carrier compatibility the Navy meant the suitability of the aircraft to fit on and work from an aircraft carrier. Three crucial parts of the carrier put limits on the size of the airplane. These counted most in determining the carrier compatibility of an aircraft: (1) the catapult and arresting gear; (2) the hangar deck; and (3) the elevators.* The catapult launched the plane; the arresting gear stopped it when landing. The amount of weight that these two devices could handle was limited. The hangar deck was where the planes were stored when not on the flight deck (the carrier's takeoff and landing strip). Since it was below the flight deck and consequently had a ceiling, the hangar deck limited the height of the plane. The elevator lifted the plane from the hangar to the flight deck. Both the weight it could lift and the length of aircraft it could accommodate were restricted.[17]

---

* A fourth characteristic helps determine carrier compatibility. It is the "spotting factor" of the aircraft; that is, the number of planes that can fit on either the flight deck or hangar deck or both. The smaller the airplane, the greater the spotting factor (the larger the number of planes that can fit on the carrier). Since an aircraft carrier never transports the maximum number of planes that it can carry, this factor puts relatively less of a limitation on the size of the aircraft. It is therefore not treated in the following discussion.

Of these three, the catapult and arresting gear were the most important for the Navy to consider when figuring carrier compatibility. The capacity of the elevators was large enough on almost all the Navy's newer carriers to handle the weight that the Air Force was seeking for the TFX. Provisions could be made for folding the tail and nose to enable the plane to fit into the hangar deck and on the elevator. But if the plane were too heavy for the catapult, it could never take off from the carrier. The Navy had an index relating the weight of the aircraft to the power of the catapult and arresting gear. It was called the "wind-over-the-deck requirement" of the aircraft. When a carrier moved through the water, it created a wind over the flight deck. If the carrier moved at 30 knots through the water, a wind of 30 knots would pass over the flight deck (assuming a dead-calm day). With a given limit to the power of the catapult and arresting gear, the wind-over-the-deck requirement of an aircraft progressed in direct proportion to its weight. That is, the heavier the plane, the more wind over the deck it would require to take off or land (the greater the wind-over-the-deck requirement). Almost all planes required some wind over the deck in order to take off and land. However, the lower the wind-over-the-deck requirement of an aircraft, the more flexibility the carrier would have in choosing courses and speeds in launching and recovering the plane.[18]

The Navy thus wanted to keep the weight of the plane as low as possible.* It wanted a plane of not more than 55,000 pounds.

* The Navy had another reason for wanting to keep the weight of the aircraft down. This one was summarized by the phrase "growth potential" of the aircraft — the amount of weight that could be added to an operational plane and still allow it to take off. The Navy had found from experience that through successive modernizations of an operational aircraft, more weight would be added to the plane. For example, a more complex and heavier missile system might replace the old one on a plane. (The weight added will usually be electronic gear or new types of armament.) Growth potential is expressed in percentages and thus refers to the percentage of original weight that can be safely added to an operational aircraft. The Navy in August of 1961, for example, was asking for a growth potential of 20 to 30 per cent for the TFX above its proposed operational weight.

The Air Force was demanding one of 75,000. The Navy also insisted that the length of the TFX must not exceed 56 feet; the Air Force wanted it to be about 70.[19] A plane without the long, narrow fuselage and great weight would not be able to give the high-low-high performance that the Air Force desired. A plane with such a narrow fuselage and great weight, however, could neither carry the radar antenna desired by the Navy nor take off from its carriers.*

The disagreement between the Air Force and Navy centered on the length, width, height, weight, range, and speed of the TFX. But, as we have said, the disagreement had a deeper meaning than these mere characteristics might suggest. The two services were fighting so hard over the physical dimensions of these characteristics because each felt its future threatened by the plane that the other wanted. The disagreement over the physical characteristics of the TFX tended to cover up the fact that each service was fighting to maintain its present or an expanded defense role for the future. The technical disagreement really represented a struggle by the Air Force and Navy to keep their identities separate, distinct, and autonomous.

The Air Force had its own military perspective. Ever since the early 1950's it had tied the mission of interdiction with tactical nuclear weapons to its tactical fighter-bombers. It had therefore built the highest performance capabilities into its fighters, like the Republic F-84, the North American F-100, and the Republic F-105.[20] For the 1950's, interdiction by fighter-bombers equipped with tactical nuclear weapons was accepted as a valid and useful mission. For the 1960's, however, the usefulness and validity of manned aircraft for such a mission were subject to serious doubts.

---

* This allegation by the Navy turned out to be incorrect, if judged by what they later accepted. The final weight of the TFX — the Navy version — was close to 70,000 pounds. The Navy said it could live with this weight. Nevertheless, in 1961, since it was taking its performance requirements from the Missileer, a considerably lighter aircraft than the TFX, the Navy kept insisting that 70,000 pounds was too much.

Missiles had downgraded the role that planes would play in either strategic nuclear retaliation or tactical nuclear interdiction. General Everest had originally conceived of the TFX as carrying only nuclear weapons because he was trying to extend the useful life of aircraft. If he could acquire an aircraft that had a nuclear capability and that had such a large ferry range and high speed on-the-deck performance, he might hope to compete with the missiles. The long ferry range would enable the plane to go nearly as far as then-existent ICBM's. The dash capability would enable the plane to escape radar detection and deliver its lethal load.

McNamara, however, wanted his new weapon systems to have both a conventional and a nuclear capability. His insistence on building a conventional capability into the TFX would have the effect of reducing its ferry range and dash performance. Under Everest's influence, the Air Force had asked that the bomb bay carry only a compact load of limited weight. This meant a nuclear weapon. A bomb bay of this design, however, was too small for the economical delivery of low-yield conventional armaments.[21] To increase their economy of delivery, the Air Force would either have to enlarge the bomb bay or add armament storage points to the wing by means of pylons. Either method would increase the takeoff weight of the TFX by increasing the number of conventional weapons it could carry. Both would reduce its ferry range. Both would also make the supersonic dash mission more costly in fuel consumption and thus reduce the distance that the plane could fly on the deck. The latter was particularly crucial to the Air Force, because the longer the plane could fly on the deck at supersonic speeds, the greater would be its chances of escaping radar detection. The dash performance was the most vital part of the high-low-high interdiction mission. To reduce the dash capability of the TFX would be equivalent to seriously crippling its interdiction capability.

If McNamara's insistence on a conventional capability for the TFX reduced its capacity for long-range interdiction, the Navy's insistence, as we have seen, on a short, fat fuselage and low weight had an added effect in the same direction. The Navy was so insistent because of its own perspectives. It had no real interest in seeing a plane built with such a long ferry range. If missiles had reduced the strategic and interdiction roles of aircraft, including naval aircraft, a plane that could fly across the Atlantic, nonstop, without refueling, and that could be deployed from semiprepared fields would be even more injurious to the Navy's interests: such a plane could only downgrade the role of the aircraft carrier. If it could fly over oceans, there would be no need to transport it over them. If it could operate from semiprepared fields, there would be less need for carriers to stand offshore to service it.[22] On the other hand, the Missileer was the ideal aircraft for the Navy. It would protect the fleet, including the aircraft carriers, from an enemy air attack. It would thereby ensure the safety of aircraft like the F-4H, which were designed to perform tactical missions from aircraft carriers.

Each service thus saw its future threatened by the other's TFX design. The Air Force wanted to extend the life of the airplane. The Navy wanted to do the same for the aircraft carrier. Both knew that the TFX program was going to be costly. Each knew that the supply of defense funds was limited. Neither wanted its future programs jeopardized by those of the other. The result of these opposing perspectives was three months of interminable discussion, delay, and disagreement.

Bargaining; Then Breakdown. The Committee on Tactical Air had issued its report entitled "Project 34" on May 19, 1961. On May 31, in a memorandum to Secretary McNamara, Secretary of the Navy John Connally expressed the Navy's concurrence in the concept of a biservice fighter. Nevertheless, he made known its strong reservations about the size and speed ranges that the Air Force was proposing for the TFX. He suggested the Navy be given the management responsibility for developing the TFX in order to ensure that it would be suitable for carrier operations.[23]

Why, however, had the Navy agreed to a biservice fighter program if it felt its future threatened by that very program? Why had it agreed to participate in the TFX program when it had its own Missileer project? The answer was simple: by the end of May the Navy no longer had the Missileer. Sometime between March and May it had been canceled.[24] The Navy thus found itself in a dilemma: it had no air-to-air superiority weapon system that could remotely compare with the Missileer, unless, of course, it chose to use the TFX. But if it did so choose, it faced the danger of procuring what it feared might be a less-than-satisfactory aircraft. The Navy tried to escape from this dilemma by doing what it did: by agreeing to the concept, though not the details, of a biservice TFX program, but also by suggesting that the Navy be the managing service rather than the Air Force. This bid, however, failed. On June 7, Secretary McNamara authorized Air Force Secretary Zuckert to develop the TFX as the follow-on to both the Air Force F-105 and the Navy F-4H. He instructed the Air Force to work closely with the Navy in order to develop a coordinated work statement, which could be issued to the aircraft industry in the fall.[25]

It appeared that the Navy now had no choice. If it wanted a follow-on air-superiority aircraft, it would have to take the TFX. But McNamara's directive had said "work closely with the Navy." Therefore, two courses of action were open to the Navy after June 7: it could refuse to lower its performance specifications and thereby preclude the possibility of a coordinated work statement; or it could lower its performance specifications to the point where it might make a coordinated work statement possible, but where its minimum performance goals would still be met. The first of these actions might end the possibility of a biservice TFX program altogether, much as the deliberations of the Committee on Tactical Air had ended the possibility of a triservice program. It might even pave the way for a restoration of the Missileer project. The second course of action would probably result in a biservice program. The Navy would not obtain its ideal fleet air defense aircraft, but its chances of receiving a satisfactory one were good.

From all the evidence, it appears that the Navy chose the first course of action.* However, whether it chose to refuse to lower its performance standards, either out of a deliberate intent to sabotage the joint program or out of an honest desire to obtain what it felt was militarily necessary if it were to perform its missions in the future, cannot be determined. Whatever its purpose, its position throughout June, July, and August almost sabotaged the program.† In intensive bargaining sessions the Navy insisted upon keeping the TFX small, its weight low, its radar antenna large, and its speed low. By early August the two services were still far apart. The Air Force demanded a fuselage length of 85 or 90 feet; the Navy, one no longer than 56 feet. The Air Force insisted that the TFX have a takeoff weight of 80,000 to 90,000 pounds, with the minimum set at 65,000. The Navy had set the maximum weight at 55,000, having compromised from its original demand of 50,000 pounds.[26]

By August 22, the two services had reached a stalemate. Both reported to the secretary of Defense that they had been unable to work out an agreement. Zuckert said the difficulty lay in the fact that the Air Force was putting priority on an offensive supersonic mission, whereas the Navy was emphasizing a subsonic

* This conclusion is based upon three things: (1) Korth's testimony before the McClellan Subcommittee (in the *TFX Hearings,* Vols. 6 and 7); (2) McNamara's decision in September of 1961 to determine unilaterally the specification guidelines (to be discussed shortly); and (3) the Navy's actions in July of 1962, in which it lowered some of its requirements (see Chapter Three).

† The explanation for the Navy's position lay in the fact that it was bargaining with the Air Force over the TFX specifications, but it was using many of the characteristics of the Missileer as its initial point of departure. The Navy may have felt that it was best to begin the bargaining by asking for its maximum goals. It could always revise these goals downward. Then again, it may have found itself caught short without any clear conception of what it should ask for in this unprecedented biservice program. It may have seized upon the Missileer's characteristics because of a lack of alternative ones. The evidence gives no proof either way.

defensive mission.[27] Acting Secretary of the Navy Fay went into more detail. He listed the problems that the Navy felt it would experience if a single compromise TFX were built:

(1) only 37 percent overall effectiveness in carrier based air-to-air combat;

(2) reduction in numbers of aircraft per aircraft carrier;

(3) increased hazards of safety of flight deck operations and personnel;

(4) increased risk in the success of the development program;

(5) higher cost of procurement and operations than are warranted; and

(6) reduced reliability and increased maintenance of the radar caused by the folding nose.[28]

In view of the increased cost, increased risk, and loss of effectiveness from a single TFX, Fay recommended:

. . . that the Air Force be authorized to proceed with the development of the Air Force TFX for its use, and that the Navy be authorized to develop, as a follow-on to the F-4H, a Navy TFX.[29]

The September Decision

McNamara's decision for commonality had come a long way in the seven months since February. He had originally wanted to develop only one tactical aircraft. In May he was forced to concede that two would be necessary. Now in August he faced the unpleasant prospect that there might very well have to be three. His reaction to this prospect was swift. If the two services could not agree between themselves on the joint specifications for the TFX, then he, McNamara, would do it for them. He instructed DDR & E to establish the guidelines under which the TFX would be jointly developed. The director, Dr. Harold Brown, delegated his task to two of his subordinates, Dr. Marvin Stern, deputy director for Weapons Systems, and A. W. Blackburn of the Tactical Weapons Office. What these two men did was to use

SOR 183 of the Air Force and modify it to take account of the Navy's requirements. In doing so, they negotiated directly with General Le May, Air Force chief of staff, and Admiral Russell, vice chief of Naval Operations.[30]

Blackburn prepared the *Memorandum of September 1* that embodied the results of their efforts. It was signed by McNamara and sent to the two service secretaries. This memorandum set forth constraints on the size of the radar dish and the bomb bay. It specified the maximum length of the aircraft, the minimum ordnance-carrying capability, and maximum takeoff weight. In it McNamara expressed his desire to achieve a common program, for he said: "Changes to the Air Force tactical version of the basic aircraft to achieve the Navy mission shall be held to a minimum."[31] To prevent any further delay, McNamara instructed the two services to ". . . convene as soon as possible to resolve differences in the pertinent detail specifications that govern the design, fabrication, performance, and testing of their respective combat aircraft."[32] Finally, if the services could not resolve the differences that remained, they were told to report them directly to the Director of Defense Research and Engineering, who would then resolve them. The *Memorandum of September 1* was thus the real starting point of the TFX as a joint program. Without it the Air Force and Navy would never have agreed on common specifications. The Memorandum provided an enforced agreement for lack of a voluntary one.

On October 1 the services sent the aircraft industry the request for proposals on the TFX and the accompanying work statement, with instructions to submit the bids by December 1, 1961. The second phase in the TFX project was over. McNamara had made his decision for commonality. The services had modified it, delayed it, opposed it, appealed it, and tried to reverse it. But in the end they failed. McNamara had enforced it. Joint specifications had been sent to industry. The question now was how industry would react. Would they or could they meet these specifications? How would their bids affect the shape of this joint program? McNamara expected to make the decision for letting the contract by February, 1962. Would the performance of industry enable him to do so?

The F-111A taking off, with wings fully extended for maximum lift.

THREE · THE THIRD PHASE: THE RUNOFF, JANUARY– NOVEMBER, 1962

During the second phase in the TFX program, there had been extensive disagreement between McNamara on the one hand and the Air Force and Navy on the other over the desirability of a joint development program. One of the reasons for this disagreement resulted from the two services' doubts about the feasibility of such a program. The variable-sweep wing to be used by the TFX would require large advances in aeronautical engineering knowledge. The services questioned the wisdom of burdening this effort with additional difficulties that would be encountered in trying to satisfy the often conflicting needs of two services. Doubts about the feasibility of a joint development program naturally strengthened (at least in the view of the Air Force and Navy) their arguments (and desires) for retaining their own separate development programs. But awareness of the technological advances that the TFX called for did not affect McNamara in the same way. He believed that the two services were using technological unknowns as an excuse for justifying years of outmoded tradition. He considered their arguments unrealistic for this reason:

the advances in technology embodied in the TFX would enable him to build a plane versatile enough to satisfy both services.[1]

The difficulty with this disagreement between McNamara and the two services was that either side could claim it was right. Or, in other words, neither side could prove that the other was wrong. No one could determine with certainty in 1961 whether such a joint project was feasible. No precedents existed for either side to appeal to, because the Defense Department had never attempted a joint development program of this size. Nor had the plane been built. Neither side, then, could deny or validate the wisdom of a joint approach. Nor could they prove or disprove the feasibility of the plane. Both the services and McNamara had to make their decisions with imperfect knowledge. As a result, these decisions were founded on judgment, not certainty. But because each side had different institutional perspectives, the decisions they did make (on August 22 and September 1, respectively) were antithetical. The services wanted to keep their development efforts separate in order to protect their autonomy. McNamara wanted to unify them in order to save money. Because he was the type of secretary of Defense he was, his decision was the one that prevailed.

His decision, however, did not end the controversy, disagreement, and opposition to a joint TFX program. It only subdued them for a brief period. They were reopened a few months later in January, 1962, when a third group entered the TFX dispute, the aircraft industry. Ultimately, only it could answer whether such a joint development project was feasible. For only it could draft the designs that would determine the suitability of the plane and only it could produce the aircraft to test its performance. If only the aircraft industry could provide the conclusive answer, however, it could do so only as the result of a process in which there would be no definitive conclusions until the very end. This was the nature of the development process. Only after the design, testing, and evaluation of the aircraft were completed could its suitability for the two services be unequivocally known. No decisions about the plane before that time could be considered certain. Therefore, McNamara and the two services would be facing throughout 1962 the same difficulty that they had faced in 1961: they would have to make decisions without being sure that they were the right ones. In 1961, they had made their respective decisions about the feasibility of a joint program without having any designs for the plane. In 1962, they would be making their decisions about the suitability of the designs but without having actual aircraft. Paper planes, not operational ones, would have to be the basis for their decisions.

In 1962, however, the decisions became even more difficult. Now it was a question not only of the suitability of the designs for a *joint* program, but also the suitability of *which* designs. McNamara was forcing the two services to decide which designs among those submitted were the most promising for a joint development program, when both services were still opposed to such a program. Of necessity the services shifted their strategy from arguing over the operational specifications each desired (McNamara had decided that for them in September of 1961) to arguing over which designs, if any, offered the best promise of providing the operational specifications that McNamara had dictated.

The unfamiliarity with the requirements of a joint development effort, the tremendous technological advances sought, the necessity to make and evaluate decisions with provisional, incomplete information, and the service opposition to a joint program — all these factors made the formal competition among the participating aircraft companies the longest ever experienced by either the services or the companies.* The competition ran for fourteen months, from October, 1961, through November, 1962. The competition lasted so long because there were in fact four separate

---

* This statement about the length of competition is true only of the System Source Selection procedure. This procedure is discussed briefly in this chapter and also in Chapter Four.

competitions or runoffs, not the customary one, among the qualified aircraft companies. The services had to conduct these four —
partly because of the deficiencies in the proposals submitted by
the aircraft companies and partly because of McNamara's insistence on correcting as many of these deficiencies as possible —
in order to decide to whom the development contract should be
awarded. The first competition ran from October, 1961, through
January, 1962; the second, from February through May, 1962; the
third, during June, 1962; and the fourth, from July through
November, 1962. The competition that received the most publicity
and the closest scrutiny from Congress was the fourth. But the
decisions on the preceding three so affected the proposals offered
by the aircraft companies and so determined the positions taken
by the military and civilian officials that we must look at them in
some detail.

However, before we do that, we must first examine the procedure under which these four competitions were carried out. For,
unless we understand this procedure — System Source Selection
— the competitions will not have much meaning. A brief discussion of the bureaucratic mechanics of System Source Selection
follows. In Chapter Four we will discuss certain other features of
this procedure.

System Source Selection

System Source Selection is a procedure through which the Air
Force under competitive conditions selects a source (a private
company familiar with and involved in defense production) to
develop its new weapon systems. System Source Selection is, then,
a technique for making decisions in the research and development
field and is applied to every significant competitive procurement
decision in this field. It is therefore used for major weapon systems (those costing a great deal in both monetary and technological resources) and for new weapon systems (those which do not

yet exist but must be developed).* The use of this technique stems from a recognition of the fact that the date of operational delivery is one of the crucial factors in determining the utility of any new weapon system. Its purpose is to save as much time as possible in the development cycle by shortening that phase of it during which the Air Force can exercise the most direct control: when a formal competition is conducted to select the most promising company. It is this period that begins with the issuance of requests for proposals to industry and ends with the announcement of the contract winner. System Source Selection is thus a technique for deciding in the shortest possible time which company will most quickly produce the required effectiveness in a proposed weapon system. The means used to save time are not important to us, but the fact that the procedure is designed to do so, is significant.

Although System Source Selection is meant to shorten the development cycle, it is also expected to increase the odds that the decisions being made are the "best" ones. It thereby represents an attempt to be as certain and as objective as possible about decisions — development decisions — that are inherently uncertain and subjective. Through System Source Selection the Air Force in effect tried to institutionalize a bias toward certainty and objectivity by constructing an elaborate procedure of evaluation, review, and re-review that every proposed major weapon system must go through before a development decision can be made. Figure 3.1 illustrates this procedure.

The first step in System Source Selection is an extensive evaluation of the proposals submitted by the aircraft companies competing for the contract.† This evaluation is performed by what the

---

* This procedure is not confined to use on *major* weapon systems alone, nor necessarily on *complete* weapon systems alone. It is usually used in some form for almost all significant procurement competitions involving the selection of sources to develop new materials. It appears to have come into use in 1956 with the Atlas ICBM program.

† Two facts should be kept in mind about the System Source Selection

Air Force calls an "Evaluation Group."[2] It consists of civilian and military employees of the Air Force, such as cost accountants, aeronautical engineers, and experienced Air Force officers, who are technically qualified to assess the proposals submitted. The size and composition of an Evaluation Group varies with each weapon system that the Air Force considers. Each Evaluation Group is in effect an ad hoc group. In the TFX case, almost 250 people were engaged in analyzing the companies' proposals. Though the size and composition of the Evaluation Group may vary, its organization usually does not. Each is divided into four sections or areas: management, operational, technical, and logistics. Each section is headed by a man called the "area cochairman." All four are under the direction of one man called the "Evaluation Group chairman." For the TFX, this man was Colonel Charles A. Gayle of the Air Force.

Each section takes every company's proposal and evaluates it from a special perspective. The management section analyzes the ability of each company to undertake and successfully complete the development of its version of the weapon system within the cost estimates and time schedules that it is proposing. To do so, the management section must determine how well the firm is managed, how realistic its cost and time estimates are, and how successful it has been in the past. The operational section analyzes the desirability of the performance features that each weapon system can be expected to offer. To do so for an airplane, it must determine the trade-offs among how far each proposed plane can fly, how fast, how high, how long, etc. The technical section analyzes the ways in which each company has solved the problem

---

procedure as it is described in the following paragraphs. First, the procedure is described as it functioned during the 1962 TFX runoff. Changes were made in this procedure in 1965, partly as a result of the 1962 TFX experience. Some of these will be discussed in Chapter Five. Second, the procedure followed for the TFX involved more levels of approval than many other source selection decisions made under this process. The TFX System Source Selection procedure was therefore more complex than most.

FIGURE 3.1 *System Source Selection Procedure*

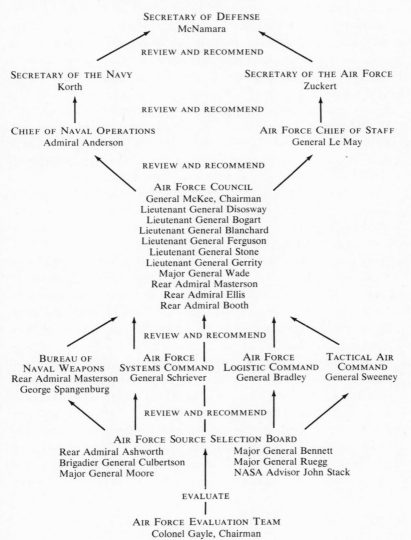

SECRETARY OF DEFENSE
McNamara

REVIEW AND RECOMMEND

SECRETARY OF THE NAVY
Korth

SECRETARY OF THE AIR FORCE
Zuckert

REVIEW AND RECOMMEND

CHIEF OF NAVAL OPERATIONS
Admiral Anderson

AIR FORCE CHIEF OF STAFF
General Le May

REVIEW AND RECOMMEND

AIR FORCE COUNCIL
General McKee, Chairman
Lieutenant General Disosway
Lieutenant General Bogart
Lieutenant General Blanchard
Lieutenant General Ferguson
Lieutenant General Stone
Lieutenant General Gerrity
Major General Wade
Rear Admiral Masterson
Rear Admiral Ellis
Rear Admiral Booth

REVIEW AND RECOMMEND

BUREAU OF
NAVAL WEAPONS
Rear Admiral Masterson
George Spangenburg

AIR FORCE
SYSTEMS COMMAND
General Schriever

AIR FORCE
LOGISTIC COMMAND
General Bradley

TACTICAL AIR
COMMAND
General Sweeney

REVIEW AND RECOMMEND

AIR FORCE SOURCE SELECTION BOARD
Rear Admiral Ashworth
Brigadier General Culbertson
Major General Moore

Major General Bennett
Major General Ruegg
NASA Advisor John Stack

EVALUATE

AIR FORCE EVALUATION TEAM
Colonel Gayle, Chairman

Source: *TFX Hearings,* Vol. 1, p. 43.

of meeting the operational specifications and thus whether in fact each company can reasonably be expected to produce the performance it has promised. To do so, it must review all the engineering aspects of each proposal to assess such things as the efficacy of the manufacturing techniques employed, the value of the types of materials required, and the feasibility of the technical approaches taken. Finally, the logistics section analyzes and tries to estimate the cost of maintaining each company's weapon system once it is operational. To do so, it must estimate things such as the numbers and types of parts that will have to be replaced and the costs involved in maintaining these parts as supply inventories. (Since the TFX was a biservice program, a fifth cochairman was added. He was Captain Shepherd from the Navy. With the aid of the Bureau of Naval Weapons, he was responsible for determining the carrier compatibility of each proposal.)

After each section has completed its analysis and evaluation of every proposal, the four area cochairmen (five for the TFX) and the Group chairman meet to determine which company has scored highest.* They do so by adding the four scores that each company achieved in each section (five for the TFX). The Evaluation Group chairman then gives to his immediate superior in the System Source Selection process these scores and the analysis supporting them. (Both are contained in the Evaluation Group Report.) His immediate superior is the Source Selection Board. Like the Evaluation Group, it is an ad hoc group. It is composed of senior representatives from the Air Force Systems Command, the Air Force Logistics Command, and the using command. The latter was the Tactical Air Command for the TFX program. Since the TFX was a biservice program, a Navy representative was added to the Board. Though there may be more than three members on the Board (four for the TFX), there are only three voting members (four for the TFX).

---

* We have examined here what each section evaluates, but not how it does so. In Chapter Four, we will discuss the method of scoring.

The Source Selection Board reviews the evaluations and technical studies of the Evaluation Group, analyzes its findings, votes in
secret to decide which company to recommend as the source, and
then sends its own recommendation, along with the Evaluation
Group Report, to the Air Force Council and to three other parties.
These are: the commander of the Air Force Systems Command;
the commander of the Air Force Logistics Command; and the
commander of the using command (TAC for the TFX). Again,
since the TFX was a biservice program, this recommendation
was sent to a fourth party, the chief of the Bureau of Naval
Weapons. Each man receives a briefing from the cochairmen.
He then determines the suitability of the recommended source for
his duties and sends his own recommendation in writing to the
Air Force Council.

The Air Force Council, established in 1951 as an agency of
the chief of staff, has developed into the senior deliberative and
advisory body for the chief of staff. It helps to formulate Air
Force objectives and to review major programs before implement-
ing them. Its members include the vice chief of staff and all the
lieutenant generals serving on the Air Staff as the various deputy
chiefs of staff. Its members thus represent all the functional elements of the Air Force. In the TFX case, three Navy personnel
were added: the deputy chief of Naval Operations for Air, the
chief of the Bureau of Naval Weapons, and the assistant chief
of the Bureau of Naval Weapons. The Air Force Council receives
an oral briefing and copies of the Evaluation Group Report from
the cochairmen of the Evaluation Group. It reviews the recommendation of the Source Selection Board, as well as those of the
various commanders. It then votes on a recommendation for a
source to develop the weapon system. The Air Force Council in
turn sends its recommendation to the Air Force chief of staff,
who either dissents or concurs, and who then sends his recommendation to the secretary of the Air Force. In a routine Air
Force procurement decision, the matter would stop here. But

because the TFX was a biservice program, a parallel course was followed in the Navy: the chief of Naval Operations received the recommendation of the Air Force Council and then sent his own to the secretary of the Navy. Finally, the two service secretaries sent their own analyses and recommendations to the secretary of Defense. It was thus he (McNamara) who made the ultimate decision.

This entire process, beginning with the intensive analysis of the Evaluation Group and ending with the decision of the secretary of Defense, comprises the slightly modified System Source Selection procedure that was followed in order to select a company to develop the TFX. Because all four competitions lasting from January through November of 1962 were carried out under this procedure, the entire gauntlet — from Evaluation Group to the secretary of Defense — had to be run every time. However, because it was not until the fourth round that he was finally presented with a *recommendation* from his service secretaries, McNamara made no *source selection* decision during the first three rounds (though he made other important decisions during them). Our examination of the first three competitions, therefore, will focus primarily on the decisions of the Source Selection Board, the Air Force Council, and the civilian secretaries.[3]

The First Competition

The requests for proposals had been issued to the aircraft industry on October 1, 1961, by the Air Force. The interested companies submitted their bids on December 1. In this first competition nine companies participated, but only six bids were offered. Three of the bids were submitted by individual companies: the Lockheed Aircraft Corporation, the North American Aviation Corporation, and the Boeing Company. The other three bids represented these team efforts: Republic Aviation and Chance Vought; General Dynamics Corporation and Grumman Aircraft; and McDonnell Aircraft and Douglas Aircraft.[4]

The Evaluation Group, after extensive analysis, concluded that none of the bids was acceptable unless substantial changes were made in all of them. This condition of the proposals probably resulted from two factors: (1) the very short time that the companies had to prepare their proposals (from October 1 to December 1, or only two months); and (2) the many unforeseen technological difficulties encountered in trying to design one plane without variations to serve the needs of two services. The Evaluation Group did find, however, that of the six bids, two were significantly better than the other four: that of the Boeing Company and that of the General Dynamics-Grumman team.[5] It recommended that paid study contracts be awarded to the two bidders so that both could eliminate the deficiencies in their proposals.

The major difficulty with the Boeing proposal was the engine it had chosen to power its version of the TFX. This engine, the General Electric MF-295, promised superior performance, lighter weight, and a smaller length and width than the other two engines approved for use on the TFX by the Air Force: the Pratt-Whitney TF-30 and the Allison AR-168. The difficulty was that the MF-295 only *promised* these desirable features; they had not yet been demonstrated. For the MF-295 was only a "paper" engine. As proposed by General Electric, it would include already developed parts of two other engines: the J-79 that powered both the Navy F-4H and the Air Force F-104 and the J-93 that would power the Air Force B-70 bomber.[6] Though both of these engines had already been tested extensively, the MF-295 had not yet been built. By January, 1962, it had progressed little beyond the design stage. It had been hurriedly designed in the latter part of the summer of 1961 when General Electric realized that none of the aircraft companies was considering using its J-79. General Electric released the MF-295 in late August — too late for the other engine manufacturers to come up with new designs before the October 1 deadline and yet early enough for General Electric to convince the military to include the MF-295 in its list of acceptable engines. The Air Force was especially pleased with this new engine. Its smaller dimensions would permit a narrower fuselage, and its superior performance and lighter weight would promise longer ferry ranges.[7] Boeing, which had been developing its designs of its variable-sweep wing aircraft around the Pratt-Whitney engine for almost two and one-half years, took a gamble and switched to the MF-295.

That gamble proved fatal. General Electric believed that the MF-295 could be developed in three years. With the date of operational delivery for the TFX set for October, 1965, the Boeing Company could not meet the timetable if it used the MF-295. But because its performance looked so promising and because the Air Force was so partial to the MF-295, Boeing, as well as North American, Lockheed, and McDonnell-Douglas, chose it.[8] However, experience had shown that designing and developing engines usually takes twice as long as it does for airframes, or about five years.[9] This would delay operational delivery for the TFX to 1967. The Evaluation Group reasoned that the advantage in superior engine performance was not worth the cost of delay in the delivery of the plane. It therefore recommended that the Boeing Company redesign its plane around another engine.

The General Dynamics-Grumman team had chosen the Pratt-Whitney TF-30 engine and had stayed with it. The Navy had already spent $30 million on its development, for the TF-30 was to be the power plant of the Missileer. It was about 300 pounds heavier than the MF-295, four inches greater in diameter, and slightly longer.[10] Despite these drawbacks, the TF-30, though not completely developed or proven, was nevertheless considerably further into the development cycle than the MF-295. The major difficulty with the General Dynamics-Grumman proposal, therefore, was not its choice of an engine but rather the carrier compatibility of its airframe design. The Evaluation Group found that the Boeing proposal was acceptable to the Navy with changes, but that the General Dynamics-Grumman design was unacceptable unless major design changes were made. The principal difficulty was a wind-over-the-deck requirement much too high for the Navy to tolerate.[11] It grossly exceeded the minimum specifications of the work statement. Because of this high requirement, the number of carriers from which the General Dynamics-Grumman TFX could operate would be severely restricted.

The Evaluation Group thus concluded that both Boeing and General Dynamics-Grumman, though their respective proposals were not acceptable, should be given paid study contracts to correct their respective deficiencies — Boeing to redesign its airframe around another engine; General Dynamics-Grumman to redesign its airframe in order to lower its wind-over-the-deck requirement. The Source Selection Board, however, did not concur completely in this evaluation. Instead it voted unanimously to recommend Boeing as the company to be selected to develop the TFX.[12] What it wanted to do, in essence, was to give a paid study contract *exclusively* to Boeing. It recognized the deficiencies in the Boeing design, but it wanted to pick a source so that the development of the plane could begin as soon as possible. Its decision thus reflected the very essence of the System Source Selection procedure: it concentrated on selecting the best source quickly, even though its design was not completely acceptable, so that the services could work closely with that one source to produce a design that would be fully acceptable. This rapid method of selecting sources would lower the costs of design competitions for industry, reduce the cost and time of evaluation for the two services, and therefore minimize the length of the formal competition.[13] The quicker a source was selected, the sooner the development of the plane could begin. To award paid study contracts to two competitors would serve only to increase costs for both industry and the services and to delay the date of operational delivery. The Source

Selection Board believed its raison d'être was to pick a source: it was instructed to do so by the regulations under which it operated. It thus did so.

The Air Force Council, however, did not have the same perspectives as the Source Selection Board. It was not an ad hoc, temporary group, but a permanent, functioning entity. Its sole reason for existence was not to select a source to develop a particular weapon system, but to review all major programs being considered by the Air Force in order to make certain that they were sensible, sound, and justifiable. The recommendation of the Source Selection Board could not help but appear to be risky, premature, and unjustifiable. The Tactical Air Command insisted the TFX be kept on the planned development schedule. The Air Force Council concluded it would be rather embarrassing to declare that Boeing had won the design competition using the MF-295 engine and then to turn around and say that it must completely redesign its winning plane because it must use a different engine. This course of action would be difficult to justify to the civilian superiors in the Defense Department. Therefore, the Air Force Council rejected the Source Selection Board's decision and concurred with the analysis of the Evaluation Group: it recommended that paid study contracts be given to Boeing and General Dynamics-Grumman. It pointed out that this course of action would produce more realistic cost estimates, would yield a final design earlier, and would save more time and dollars in the long run.[14]

The secretaries of the Navy and Air Force agreed with the decision of the Air Force Council. In a written statement to McNamara, Korth and Zuckert pointed out the reasons for their decision. They said:

> (1) the proposals of the two companies were markedly superior to the others and offered the best chance of being brought up to the stated service requirements;
> (2) the services were unanimous in rejecting the G.E. en-

gine . . . because of the low probability of its development in the time required, since not even a prototype existed. . . .

(3) the extension would permit the fuller use of the two designs and provide the incentive for sharper competition from business and design standpoints.[15]

McNamara agreed with Korth and Zuckert. He directed them to award two paid study contracts, one to the Boeing Company and one to the General Dynamics-Grumman team. These contracts would last from sixty to ninety days, beginning from January 31. The two finalists would have to complete their additional efforts by May 1.

The Second Competition

Both competitors worked hard during February and March to correct the deficiencies in their respective proposals. Boeing redrew its design around the Pratt-Whitney TF-30 engine.* The General Dynamics-Grumman team attempted to increase the carrier compatibility of its design by reducing its wind-over-the-deck requirement. Both competitors submitted their second proposals on April 2. The Evaluation Group analyzed these new proposals during April and the early part of May. On May 14 the Source Selection Board met to consider the two new bids. The three voting Air Force members concluded that the Boeing proposal was the better one. They decided the General Dynamics-Grumman plane had a center of gravity shift (due to the sweeping of the wings) so undesirable that the performance of the plane would be seriously degraded.[16] The voting Navy member agreed with these two conclusions, but he still considered neither design acceptable

---

* Actually, the Defense Department civilian officials had directed the Boeing Company to use the Pratt-Whitney engine. They had, however, encountered strong objections from high-level Air Force officers. The latter objected to being told to use a Navy-developed engine and to having it produced in a Navy-controlled plant. The Air Force still considered the MF-295 the best engine. Resentment over this incident only increased the original hostility of the Air Force toward the biservice program.

to the Navy. By a vote of three to one, the Source Selection Board recommended for the second time that Boeing be picked as the source to develop the TFX. On May 24, the Air Force Council met. The seven Air Force and three Navy officers all agreed that Boeing offered the superior proposal. But though they all recommended that Boeing be selected as the source, the Navy representatives refused to approve its design as acceptable.[17]

Thus the Navy had twice expressed its opinion that the Boeing design would not fulfill its service requirements. As a result, even if Boeing were chosen as the source, work on the biservice plane could not begin. The Navy had first to accept the Boeing design. The difficulty that the two services were experiencing here was caused in large part by their differing philosophies on how to select companies to develop weapons. Under the System Source Selection procedure the Air Force put the emphasis on selecting the most promising source as quickly as possible, even if its designs were not completely satisfactory. Then it would sit down with this source and work out the design changes that were necessary to produce a fully satisfactory design.[18] The purpose of this method was, of course, to save time. The Navy, on the other hand, put the major emphasis on the design. The source was secondary. What was essential was to secure a design as detailed and as nearly perfected as possible *before* the Navy would commit itself to a source. In this way there would be a minimum of uncertainty as to whether it was technically feasible for the chosen design to meet the military specifications.*

However, since the TFX was a biservice program and since the

---

* The Navy could afford to concentrate on designs first and sources second. For the Navy works with a small group of aircraft companies that have gained much experience in meeting Navy specifications and that have proven themselves to be reliable sources. These companies are generally equal in their capabilities. The Navy can thus afford to put its emphasis on designs first because it does not have to concern itself with the qualifications of the sources offering the designs. The Air Force, however, does not work with such a small or uniformly qualified group.

Air Force had the responsibility and authority for managing this program, the Navy was forced to participate in the Air Force method of selecting companies to develop weapons. Although it participated in the System Source Selection process, the Navy did not completely adopt it. The Navy went along with Air Force procedure in selecting the source rather than the design first. But it refused to commit itself to the development program until it had assured itself that the *design* of the source chosen was satisfactory for its own specifications.[19] The Navy did not want to agree to a program on the basis of incomplete designs and then find out several months later that the final design had sacrificed its requirements. It wanted a guarantee that its interests would be protected. Since only about a sixth of these planes were being constructed for the Navy, this tactic was probably a wise one. The Navy was using what little leverage it still had to its best advantage. Since McNamara had made it clear to the Air Force that the only way it would obtain a TFX was through a biservice program, the Navy literally held a veto over the TFX. It could threaten the entire program with collapse unless it could be convinced that its interests were being met. The only way it could be so convinced was to see designs that accommodated its special requirements.

By May of 1962, the Navy had not yet seen any such designs. Neither the Boeing Company's proposal nor that of the General Dynamics-Grumman team fulfilled its carrier compatibility specifications. In this area the Boeing design had deteriorated from the first to the second evaluation. Because it had to redesign its plane around the heavier Pratt-Whitney engine, the gross weight of its plane had increased by 4,000 pounds.[20] As a result, the Boeing design now had an unacceptably high wind-over-the-deck requirement. If the Boeing design deteriorated, that of its competitor improved. The General Dynamics-Grumman design, however, still had too high a wind-over-the-deck requirement.[21] One or both of two things would have to be done if either design were to become suitable: either the weight of the plane would have to be reduced or the area of the wing increased.* Both actions would lower the wind-over-the-deck requirement to an acceptable figure. Either action, however, would degrade the supersonic dash capability the Air Force wanted.

The Air Force and the Navy were thus again at a stalemate, this time in late May, 1962. Part of the problem resulted from their different philosophies on how best to procure a weapon system, but another factor was equally significant: both competitors had found it impossible to design in *one* plane the features that would meet the requirements set by the Air Force and Navy. For the first and second competitions no *structural* divergence was permitted.† Each competitor had submitted two structurally identical designs to fulfill the missions of both services.[22]

Whatever the reasons, the Navy was preparing to recommend that the biservice effort be terminated. On May 16, the chief of the Bureau of Naval Weapons (Admiral Stroop) sent a recommendation to the chief of Naval Operations (Admiral Anderson). In it he stated that his office felt the chances of obtaining a successful biservice plane were remote, and he advised against further efforts to achieve such a plane.[23] In his recommendation to the secretary of the Navy, Admiral Anderson stated that he had "no indication that Navy requirements can indeed be met" and in effect suggested abandoning the efforts to achieve a joint fighter.[24] A memorandum was then prepared for Secretary Korth's signa-

* Reducing the weight, however, might prove difficult. At this time the Air Force had reduced its weight requirement from 85,000 to 65,000 pounds. But the Navy insisted that the plane be no heavier than 55,000 pounds. There was still a difference of 10,000 pounds between the two services' positions, almost nine months after McNamara had supposedly settled the issue of weight by his September 1, 1961 Memorandum.

† When I say that no *structural* divergence was permitted, I do not mean to imply that only one version of the plane was offered for the two services. There were two versions, one for each service. However, the two versions were *structurally* identical; that is, their airframes (that part of the plane including the wings, fuselage, and tail) were identical. The differences between the two versions of each design were in component parts, such as electronic equipment and armament.

ture, stating that the Navy could not use the two designs and recommending that the Air Force be allowed to proceed independently with a TFX for its own use. The deputy chief of Naval Operations, Admiral Pirie, got wind of this memorandum. It was pointed out to him that Secretary McNamara had already decided to proceed with a joint development program and therefore that the only way the Navy could hope to obtain a fighter for fleet air defense was to participate in the program. Such a position as advocated in the memorandum could at best only be expected to delay the program, but not end it. Admiral Pirie thereupon contacted officials in the Air Force and convinced them that more attention should be paid to the Navy's requirements.[25]

This memorandum was never signed by Korth. Instead, both he and Zuckert recommended to Secretary McNamara that the two competitors be given additional time so that they could try to provide satisfactory solutions to the Navy's objections. The two secretaries suggested that three weeks would be enough time for them to remedy the deficiencies. Then they pointed out that two structurally identical aircraft could not meet the requirements of both services. They therefore recommended that some divergence in the airframe structure be permitted in the two versions. Only in this way, they said, would it be possible to continue with the joint development program. They would, however, instruct the two competitors that they must keep this divergence to an absolute minimum.[26]

The two service secretaries thus asked McNamara to yield again on his directions for a joint program. In February of 1961, he had decided to develop three structurally identical planes in order to satisfy the tactical fighter needs of all the services. In May of 1961, he was forced to concede that two entirely different planes would be necessary for the services. In September of 1961, he had quelled an incipient revolt by the Air Force and Navy by unilaterally deciding on the structural characteristics for the one plane that would serve them both. Now, in May of 1962, he was being confronted with the prospect that his September decision might be reversed: that the Air Force and Navy might in fact obtain their own, separate planes. By permitting some divergence in the structural design, he faced the danger of reopening the door to two separate planes that he had closed nine months before.

Upon receiving these two recommendations for granting another runoff and for permitting some divergence, McNamara instructed his office to do a detailed analysis. The conclusion he received was that steps could be taken to reduce the weight of the Navy version without generating structural differences so large between it and the Air Force version that the inherent savings of a joint program would be lost.[27] On June 9, McNamara concurred with Korth's and Zuckert's two recommendations and authorized the third competition. He insisted, however, that the differences between the two versions be kept to a minimum.

The Third Competition

The third competition lasted only three weeks. The two competitors consequently had less than two weeks to correct their deficiencies for the Navy. They submitted their third designs to the Evaluation Group on June 15. This group had only five days to analyze and assess the new designs, for the Source Selection Board met on June 20 to consider them.[28] Its members found that the Boeing Company had produced a substantially better plane than it had submitted during the second round. It had increased the wing area of the plane by 15 per cent. The Navy especially welcomed this increase: it reduced the wind-over-the-deck requirement and lengthened the loitering capability. Though the larger wing area reduced somewhat the supersonic dash capability of its version, the Air Force concluded it received an acceptable trade-off, because it obtained longer ferry ranges and a larger ordnance-carrying capability.[29] The Source Selection Board members were less pleased with the submission of the General

Dynamics-Grumman team. It had offered for its Air Force version the same design that it had submitted in the second round. But it had presented six new possible designs for the Navy version. Two of these it had selected as the most desirable. One would have combined an entirely new Navy wing with the Air Force fuselage; the other, an entirely new Navy fuselage with the Air Force wing.[30] The Source Selection Board recommended for the third time that Boeing be selected as the source to develop the TFX because it had presented the superior design.

On June 21, the Air Force Council met. It unanimously recommended that Boeing be selected to develop the TFX. It concluded that this finding was unequivocal. It agreed that the choice of the source was not an issue. And it stated that the definition of the design should follow the selection of the source. The Navy representatives on the Council were willing to and did concur with all these statements. They agreed that the choice of the source was not an issue because they too concluded that Boeing offered the superior proposal. They agreed that this finding was unequivocal. They recommended that Boeing be selected. But these were not the crucial issues for the Navy men. For, though they now agreed that the definition of the design should follow the selection of the source, the Navy representatives refused to commit their service unequivocally to proceeding with this program until *after* the design had been defined. The chief of Naval Operations, Admiral Anderson, therefore recommended that only the Boeing Company be selected to continue design studies.[31]

The reason the Navy refused to commit itself to the joint program was due to the nature of the third competition: it was far too short. The Boeing Company had not had time to validate its new designs by extensive wind-tunnel testing. Nor had the Navy itself had time to validate the designs: the Boeing proposals were not fully documented and the evaluation period was much too short (only five days).[32] Thus the Navy, because of its procurement practices and because of the fear that its interests would be sacrificed, again produced an inconclusive result. In May the Navy had refused to proceed with the joint program because neither design was then acceptable. Now in June, when one design *looked* acceptable, the Navy was refusing because this service was not convinced that it actually *was* acceptable.

Both the Source Selection Board and the Air Force Council agreed with the Navy position. In their recommendations they noted that the extremely short time available had precluded obtaining enough contractor and Evaluation Group data to determine the ultimate acceptability of the design changes for the Navy's requirements. The secretary of the Air Force and the secretary of the Navy concurred in this finding. But, whereas the chief of Naval Operations and the chief of staff of the Air Force had recommended that only Boeing be selected to continue defining its design, the two service secretaries recommended that both the Boeing Company and the General Dynamics-Grumman team be allowed to do so.[33] They suggested giving still another paid study contract to these two competitors. Each would receive $2.5 million for 60 days of study. An evaluation period of 45 days would then follow.

Secretary McNamara backed the recommendation of his two service secretaries. He authorized a fourth and final competition in order to define further the designs so that their acceptability for the services' requirements could be determined. He had two additional motives in authorizing a fourth competition: (1) he wanted to obtain more realistic estimates on the total cost of the development program, for he felt that the costs that each competitor was presenting were much too low; and (2) he wanted to maximize the similarities in the two versions of the plane, for he felt that the divergencies in the respective designs offered by the two competitors were much too large.[34] McNamara, however, preferred to give not one but two contracts because he reasoned he was more likely to obtain these two results from the pressures of a competitive environment.

74

The Fourth Competition

The fourth competition began on July 1, but under a new rule that made it quite different from the other three. This new rule allowed the Evaluation Group to work with each competitor as if he were a prime contractor. In the three previous exercises, the companies were presented with the performance specifications that the services had drawn up. They then prepared to the best of their ability designs that would meet those specifications. They were not helped in any way by the Evaluation Group in producing their designs. This was standard Air Force procedure. Because the companies were competing with each other, the Air Force personnel remained uninvolved in order to determine objectively which company produced the best design. The competitive nature of these exercises required the strictest neutrality on the part of the Air Force.

Three competitions, however, had failed to produce even one design completely satisfactory to both services. In order to ensure that this would not happen again, Secretary McNamara instructed Zuckert to authorize Colonel Gayle to work closely with each competitor as if he were the prime contractor — that is, as if he had already won the competition and now all that remained for him to do was to touch up and finalize the design.[35] In other words, Gayle could work with each competitor as if he were the source chosen to develop the TFX.* Since "pure" competition had not yielded a satisfactory design, the Air Force would rig this runoff so that it would. Gayle was therefore permitted to identify the deficiencies in each design during the competition, not after it was over, as was customary. He could also suggest specific ways of correcting the deficiencies, including the materials to be used. The one thing he could not do was to design the plane for each competitor. Although he could suggest ways of correcting their

* Colonel Gayle had been urging his superiors for several months to allow him to do this.

deficiencies, he could not tell them which to use or which was the best to use.[36] His only task was to locate weak spots and list ways of remedying them. To do so, Gayle gave each competitor a document that outlined his respective faults. He then sat down with each separately and periodically to review the results of his efforts. In order to maintain his impartiality, he never revealed to one competitor the designs or processes of the other; nor did he make information available to one that was not also given to the other.

Moreover, in order to make certain that he would receive what he wanted in these designs, McNamara told the two competitors exactly what he was looking for, through his deputy secretary of Defense, Roswell Gilpatric. The latter wrote to the presidents of the Boeing Company, Grumman Aircraft, and the General Dynamics Corporation. In his letter of July 13, he stated explicitly the three conditions that had to be met before any contract would be awarded:

> (1) Satisfaction of both the Navy and Air Force that a significant improvement to their tactical air capabilities is represented by the winning design.
>
> (2) Minimum divergence from a common design compatible with the separate missions of the Air Force and Navy to protect the inherent savings of a joint program.
>
> (3) Demonstrably credible understanding of costs both for development and procurement of the complete TFX weapon system, which costs must be acceptable in view of the capability added to our military strength by the weapon system.[37]

McNamara thus revealed to the two competitors the areas on which he would focus in judging and comparing their proposals: the acceptability to the services of the plane's operational capability, the degree of commonality of the design, and the realism of the cost estimates.

During the sixty days of paid study, the General Dynamics-Grumman team made great strides in advancing the quality of its designs. It did so because it had developed a new process for constructing small-scale test models of planes. Previously it had forged its models from stainless steel. This method required from six weeks to two months to produce a finished model. Now the team began casting its models from fiberglass and could produce a finished model in less than ten days.[38] This breakthrough in model building was crucial to the team's large advances. For it was on these models that the engineers would conduct their wind-tunnel experiments. From the results collected from these experiments, they would test and improve the designs of the aircraft. Obviously, the more quickly they could build models, the more wind-tunnel experiments they could conduct and the faster they could correct the deficiencies in their designs.

On September 11, the two competitors turned in their fourth and final proposals. On October 15, Admiral Anderson reported that the Bureau of Naval Weapons had found both designs acceptable. On November 2, Colonel Gayle reported to the Source Selection Board that the Evaluation Group had found both designs acceptable. On November 2, the Source Selection Board voted unanimously to recommend the Boeing Company. On November 2, General Bradley, commander of the Air Force Logistics Command, concurred in the selection of the Boeing Company. On November 2, General Sweeney, commander of the Tactical Air Command, also concurred. On November 6, General Schriever, commander of the Air Force Systems Command, and Admiral Masterson, chief of the Bureau of Naval Weapons, both did likewise. On November 8, the Air Force Council of six lieutenant generals, one major general, one full general, and three admirals voted unanimously to recommend Boeing as the source to develop the TFX. Within the next few days the chief of Naval Operations, Admiral Anderson, and the chief of staff of the Air Force, General Le May, endorsed this recommendation.[39] In the fourth evaluation there was thus unanimity — absolutely no dissent — up through the entire military chain of command, in recommending the Boeing Company.

Then on November 13, Secretary of Defense McNamara had his usual weekly breakfast with Deputy Secretary of Defense Gilpatric, Secretary of the Air Force Zuckert, and Assistant Secretary of the Navy for Research and Development, Dr. Wakelin. On November 21, the Pentagon publicly announced that the General Dynamics-Grumman team had received the contract to produce 22 prototype F-111's (TFX's) at a cost of $439 million. McNamara had thus overruled the unanimous recommendation of one colonel, four major generals, six lieutenant generals, five generals, five rear admirals, and one admiral.

The question remains: why did he do it? Why did he decide as he did?

PART II · THE EVALUATION

In its four-year history, the TFX program had undergone several major changes. The Air Force had begun it as a single-service project early in 1959. It had remained so until McNamara came to the Defense Department in 1961. In February of that year he had decided to reorient this single-service program into a tri-service one. Three months later, in May, he had been forced by the services' opposition to change the TFX into a biservice program. Three months later, in August, he had been faced with the prospect that Air Force and Navy opposition would destroy even a biservice effort. In September, he alone had saved the program by deciding for the two services what they had been unable or unwilling to decide for themselves. Eight months later, in May of 1962, he had once again to face the fact that the TFX as a biservice program was on the verge of total collapse because of service opposition. He alone had again saved the biservice feature of the program by allowing each of the two services to have its own version of the TFX.

Therefore, at least one constant theme in the TFX story runs throughout the two years during which McNamara was involved with it: he encountered immediate and continuous service opposition to every decision he made; and as a result, he was forced periodically to reduce the scope of the program. By May of 1962, the services had succeeded in whittling down McNamara's original plans for a triservice fighter so far that he was beginning to question whether the TFX was still a biservice one. The TFX program, then, was controversial even before McNamara overruled his military advisors in November, 1962. Its whole history was characterized by continual turbulence and dissension.

The TFX was such a program because McNamara was asking the military services to do something that few civilian secretaries had ever asked, much less required of them: he demanded that they combine their separate development programs (for tactical fighters) into one common program. He was forcing them, in effect, to partake in the dismantling of their separate service identities. For the services the TFX in 1961–62 posed the same threat to their right to individual development programs that the unified and specified commands had posed in 1958 to their right to supreme operational command authority. (The measures in 1958 had increased the operational command authority of the Joint Chiefs of Staff by reducing that of the three services.) If McNamara succeeded in keeping the TFX a biservice program, he might lay the basis for a pattern that would increase the already large powers of the Office of the Secretary of Defense over the services' development programs. A loss of independent decision-making power to a more centralized, superior civilian authority might mean the end of all effective service initiative in the field of weapons development. If the unified and specified commands had brought greater integration of the services at the output end of the Pentagon, then the TFX threatened to hasten this already prevalent trend at the input end. Both kinds of integration were feared by the services because they wanted to protect and maintain their individual autonomy.

Integration in the field of developing new weapon systems, however, hit the services where it hurt them most. For it was here that they could best hope to combat the trend toward the centralization of power in the Office of the Secretary of Defense and perhaps even hope to reverse it. If each service could retain control over its own development programs, it could still hope to carve out its own exclusive domain for the future. Sole ownership of a unique weapon might mean more autonomy at the best and more bargaining power at the worst. But if the services were forced to participate in common development programs — and the TFX meant exactly that — then their best chance of resisting both the trend toward integration and the concomitant increasing power of the secretary of Defense would be lost.

If this discussion explains why the TFX was a controversial program, it does not explain why McNamara's November 21 announcement was a controversial decision. But it does give a clue. Just as McNamara was trying to force the services into accepting a common development program, so too was he trying to change the bases on which they had traditionally made their decisions in their own programs. Just as the joint nature of the program was new, so too were the factors on which he was asking them to select the winning bid. It was not that he was asking them to forget completely the promised operational performance of the planes. Rather, it was that he was asking them to give more consideration than they had to realistic cost estimates and to the similarities of the designs. The services were uncomfortable with both — uncomfortable with cost realism because they had not been accustomed to thinking in a cost-effectiveness manner and uncomfortable with commonality because they were opposed to it.

The reason why the military officers in the fourth evaluation were unanimous in recommending the Boeing Company was that they were all putting the *same* emphasis on the *same* factors in order to make their decision. They *did* think alike in this instance. The fact that McNamara overruled their recommendation suggests

81

that he did not agree with their thinking. Therefore, in order to explain McNamara's decision, we must do three things: first, show what were the criteria he used in making his decision; second, show how these criteria differed from those of the military; and third, show why he used them. Chapter Five will perform the first and second tasks; Chapter Four, the third.

The F-111A, carrying training weapons on pylons that swivel to keep the weapons parallel to the flight path when the wings are swept back.

FOUR · TWO PROBLEMS IN RESEARCH AND DEVELOPMENT PROCUREMENT

To explain why McNamara used the criteria he did before explaining what they were may seem to be putting the two in reverse order. Actually we are not doing so. In explaining why McNamara chose the criteria he did in order to make his decision, we do not have to deal directly with them. It is his approach to development problems generally, not his approach to this specific problem, which will absorb us here. In other words, the *reasons* why he chose to emphasize the factors that he did in the TFX case, not the factors themselves (to be discussed in Chapter Five), are the subject of this chapter.

The reasons he had reflect a predetermined method of approaching the inherent difficulties of the development process. To discover McNamara's method of dealing with these difficulties, we must do two things: (1) discuss the problem of optimism in the bidder's estimates of development costs; and (2) examine a particular problem associated with the System Source Selection process, namely, the lack of freedom for the civilian service secretary in exercising his statutory right to choose among alternative devel-

opment programs. The first is common to all development programs; the second is peculiar to those of the Air Force. The first
will help to explain why McNamara chose the criteria he did; the
second, why he rejected those of the military.

Cost Optimism

Defining the Problem of Cost Optimism. The expression "cost
optimism" refers to the phenomenon of the federal government
usually paying a company much more to develop a weapon system
than the company had originally told the government it would cost.
Optimism in a bidder's cost proposal is the difference between the
early estimated cost and the final or actual cost. The former is
usually much lower than the latter. Of the three variables in the development of any weapon system — cost of development, length
(time) of development, and performance (the quality) of the
system — it is usually the cost estimate that turns out to be the
most unrealistic because it has been the most underestimated.
Because the premium has been placed first on the quality of the
weapon system and next on the date of operational delivery, it is
the target cost that is and must be neglected when unforeseen
technological and other difficulties occur. In their sampling of the
development programs for twelve major weapon systems, Peck and
Scherer found, for example, that the average cost variance was 3.2.
That is, it cost 220 per cent more to develop the weapon than
originally predicted. The time variance was only 1.36 (it took 36
per cent longer to develop the system than originally predicted).
The performance standards were almost always met.[1] Thus the
unpredictability and uncertainty inherent in developing a weapon
system manifest themselves most severely in the cost area.

Cost optimism is a problem for the government because it is
expensive: the government finds itself paying more than it had
bargained for. This in itself is a waste of resources. But it can
cause much more serious trouble by leading the government into

making unsound development decisions. In cost-effectiveness terms the government may have been forced to spend more on developing a weapon system because of faulty cost estimates than its military effectiveness warranted. The government may have decided that it could have spent the money more effectively elsewhere had it known the actual cost. Cost optimism can lead to an inefficient allocation of scarce resources.

Cost optimism has always been a problem in developing advanced new weapon systems. When there are so many uncertainties over both the kind and number of the technological difficulties that will be encountered, it is understandably difficult to predict costs precisely. Two factors, however, have made cost optimism a much greater problem than it was in the past. First, the absolute size of defense spending on research and development (R & D) has increased dramatically. In 1945, defense spending on R & D totaled $500 million. In 1953, this figure had risen to $2.4 billion. By 1963, it had nearly trebled, reaching $7 billion.[2] R & D expenditures have risen from less than 5 per cent to nearly 20 per cent of total annual defense spending.[3] Second, the size of the R & D expenditure in relation to the total expenditure on a particular weapon system has been increasing.* Table 4.1 gives some idea of the increase of R & D spending as a proportion of respective total expenditures on selected weapon systems. The large absolute and proportional increases in R & D expenditures have resulted from several factors: the increasing complexity of modern weapons, the decline (both in physical numbers and dollar amounts) of their production runs, and the rapid obsolescence of these advanced weapons.

Whatever the causes of these two increases in R & D spending, the very fact that they have made the annual total expenditure for

_____

* The total expenditure on a weapon system is that incurred during its life cycle. The latter stretches from the time the system is first conceived on the drawing boards until the time it is phased out of use. Total expenditure thus includes the cost of development, production, and maintenance.

TABLE 4.1. *R & D Spending per Weapon System*
(figures in percentages)

System	R & D	Investment[a]	Operation	Total
B-36	2	25	73	100
B-47	3	47	50	100
B-52	5	50	45	100
B-58	18	52	30	100
B-70 (small force)	30	43	27	100
B-70 (large force)	12	45	43	100
F-86	1	23	76	100
F-100	3	39	58	100
F-105	21	49	30	100
F-108	23	42	35	100

[a] Production.

Source: David Novick, *Identifying R & D: A Management Problem,* RAND Paper 2135 (Santa Monica, Calif.: The RAND Corporation, 1960), p. 10.

developing weapon systems so large has posed new dangers. Cost optimism can have many more detrimental effects on the national defense effort when the development sums involved are so large. Because R & D expenditures have become a much larger part of both the total defense budget and each major new weapon system, the risks of waste and inefficient allocation of resources have become greater. Thus behind any effort to maximize the military effectiveness of defense spending, while minimizing its cost, must lie an attempt to produce more realistic cost estimates for development programs. This is exactly what McNamara had decided to do after entering the Defense Department.

McNamara's Methods of Dealing with Cost Optimism. Because the trend had been toward larger expenditures during the most uncertain phase of the life cycle of a weapon system (the development as opposed to either the production or maintenance phase), McNamara felt the problem of developmental cost optimism to be a grave one. He searched for ways of dealing with this problem, calling for more imaginative Department of Defense (DOD) procedures that would force industry's cost bids to be more realistic than they had been. One of the methods that he hit upon was the following: in contracting for the development of advanced weapon systems, he would increase the number of incentive contracts and reduce the number of the cost reimbursement type. McNamara realized that part of the blame for cost optimism lay with the government: because it did not employ the types of contracts that rewarded realism and penalized optimism, the government could not and should not expect to receive realistic bids.

Throughout the 1940's and 1950's, the government had used the cost-plus-fixed-fee contract (CPFF) in the majority of its development programs for advanced weapon systems. Under the CPFF contract, the buyer (the government) and the seller (the contracting company) agreed on a fee (the profit) that was based on an estimate of the total cost of the development program (the target cost). The target cost, however, was not binding on the seller because the buyer agreed to reimburse the seller for all costs incurred by him in fulfilling the contract. The seller thus had no contractual incentive to minimize his actual incurred costs both because the government paid them all and because he was guaranteed a fixed fee no matter how large the final costs of the program were.[4] The seller also had no contractual incentive to minimize his cost *estimates*. In fact, if there were any incentive, it was for him to maximize them — to make his estimates as large as possible while remaining competitive with the other bidding firms. This was so because in practice the fee was determined as a percentage of the target cost. The larger he made his target cost, the greater the profit the seller stood to receive.[5]

Thus the contractual incentives for cost reduction and cost realism were at a minimum under the CPFF contract. But so was the risk for the industrial contractor. For both industry and government, especially during the Eisenhower administration, believed that innovation and invention could not be costed. Contractors refused to undertake development programs unless they were protected by the CPFF contract. They argued that the uncertainties

89

inherent in development precluded the possibility of accurate cost estimates. They did not want to assume the financial risks created by these uncertainties. The government acquiesced in CPFF contracting for two reasons: (1) it could thereby maintain strict control over the company's development efforts (since the company had to submit all new, unforeseen costs to the government for approval under this type of contract); and (2) the government often wanted to begin full-scale efforts on crash projects as soon as possible; with little information on the feasibility of new weapons, companies would undertake the project only if the government guaranteed to bear the costs.[6] As a result of this mutual agreement, as the volume of expenditures on R & D increased, so did the number of CPFF contracts. In fiscal year 1952, for example, 4.9 per cent of the total number of procurement actions (including development and production) were of the cost reimbursement type; in dollars, the figure was 12.7 per cent. In fiscal year 1959 these figures had risen to 15.4 per cent and 40.9 per cent, respectively.[7] Thus during the 1950's, because the amounts the government committed to development programs skyrocketed, so did the use of CPFF contracts.

McNamara's reasoning, however, differed from that of his predecessors at the Pentagon. If they believed the best and quickest way to obtain a quality weapon system was for the government to assume the risks, he felt that the "best" way for the government to misallocate resources was for it to do precisely that — to assume all the risks. Moreover, he believed he could obtain all three — a quality system in the shortest possible time with the government bearing as little risk as possible — if he would use the incentive type of contract. Under that contract, cost optimism would be automatically penalized, whereas meeting target costs, time schedules, and performance goals would be automatically rewarded.

Several types of incentive contracts were available for him to use. The one that promised to yield the strongest spur to industry to meet the time, cost, and quality goals and that promised to present the government with the least risk was the firm-fixed-price contract (FFP). The FFP contract was at the opposite pole from the CPFF contract: if the government bore all the financial risks of development under the CPFF contract, it would bear almost none under the FFP type. Under this contract, the seller would agree to develop a weapon system at a price that, once negotiated, would remain fixed. The price could not be revised upward (or downward) to reflect changes in the seller's estimates of his costs or his experience in incurring them. Thus, under the FFP contract, because the price remained fixed, the profit would be the residual of price less costs.[8] Because costs and profit were inversely related, the seller would have a strong contractual incentive to keep his costs as low as possible. In this way he could maximize his profits. For the same reason he would have strong contractual incentives to estimate his costs as accurately as possible. If he underestimated them and consequently incurred greater costs than planned, then he and not the government would be the one to pay them. His profits would be correspondingly reduced.

Thus if the incentives for cost reduction and cost realism were at a minimum under the CPFF contract, they would be at a maximum under the FFP type. Between these extremes lay many kinds of contracts that promised different incentives for achieving cost realism and reduction, depending upon their respective terms. McNamara chose one for the TFX development contract that provided incentives for cost realism and economy almost as strong as those set up by the FFP types. This was the fixed-price-incentive-fee contract (FPIF).* Under this type, the seller would estimate his total costs (his target cost). Included as a part of the target cost would be the profit he expected to make (his target profit).

---

* The FFP contract is too rigid for development programs. It takes no account of the uncertainties inherent in research and development. It makes the company assume the entire financial burden. There is enough (legitimate) uncertainty in developing weapon systems to warrant some inaccuracy in estimating costs. The FPIF contract allows for this uncertainty.

The Evaluation

Depending upon the contract, the government would set an upper limit to the price it would pay the contractor to develop the weapon system. This would be called the ceiling price and would be expressed as a percentage of the target cost.[9] For example, the ceiling price for the TFX contract was 120 per cent of the contractor's target cost. If the target cost were $100 million, the most the government would pay would be $120 million.* Any costs above that would have to be borne entirely by the seller; that is, he would pay 100 per cent of the costs above the ceiling price.

For cost overruns between the contractor's target cost and the government's ceiling price, a sharing formula would be negotiated. Under this arrangement the government and the company would agree to share any of the overruns according to a predetermined percentage. For the TFX development contract, the sharing formula was 90-10 per cent.[10] If the target cost were $100 million, the ceiling price $120 million, and the overrun $10 million (the total price for the contract being $110 million), the government would pay $9 million and the company $1 million. But the sharing formula would work in the same way for cost underruns. If the contractor succeeded in developing the weapon for $90 million, the government would deduct $9 million from the price it would pay and the company would add $1 million to its profits.

Thus under the FPIF contract the major incentive for realism

---

* The target cost for the TFX development contract was $439,380,000, not $100,000,000. The latter figure is used to illustrate the point more clearly. The ceiling price for the TFX development contract was $527,256,000. These are the figures of *Letter Contract No. AF 33(657)-8260* between the Department of the Air Force and the General Dynamics Corporation for twenty-two F-111 aircraft, signed on December 19, 1962. This target cost did not include the Pratt-Whitney engines, the Hughes Phoenix Missile System, spare parts, aerospace ground equipment, or training parts. (A letter contract is one that gives the contractor authority to begin development, but it does not fully define what the weapon system will look like when development has been completed. Because it often takes a year for the service and the contractor to agree exactly on what the one wants and the other is producing, a letter contract is issued to enable the contractor to begin work.)

in cost estimates would be the binding nature of the ceiling price; the major incentive for cost reduction, the sharing formula. The ceiling price would mean that the contractor would have to pay heavily if his mistakes in estimating costs (deliberate or otherwise) were large. He would have only a 20 per cent leeway, not 220 per cent. The sharing formula would mean that there would be no limit to his profits. The larger his underrun, the greater his profits. The government too would benefit from the FPIF contract. Not only would there be an upper legal limit to the price it would pay, but also there would be no contractual limit to the money it could save. Under the FPIF contract the seller, not the government, would have to assume the major financial burden of the development risks.

McNamara, therefore, had two reasons for making greater use of incentive contracting. First, he wanted to lower the prices that the government had to pay for research and development. He would do so by forcing the contractor to minimize his actual costs. Second, he desired to reduce the number of faulty decisions that caused resources to be misallocated. He would do so by forcing the contractor to be more realistic in his estimates of developmental costs.* However, if the incentive contract would force the defense contractor to try to be more realistic in his cost estimates and more economy-minded in his development programs, it would not necessarily aid him in doing so. For with the widespread use of the CPFF contract in the 1950's, neither the government nor industry had developed methods with which they could reliably predict and then monitor development costs. Without the aid of effective management techniques, the government found it difficult to assess the realism (or optimism) of the contractor's estimates. The contractor, because he was not forced to be realistic,

* McNamara was successful in reducing CPFF contracting and increasing the incentive type. From a peak of 38 per cent during the first nine months of fiscal year 1961, he had lowered CPFF contracting to 32.5 per cent of the total dollar volume by the end of fiscal year 1962.

did not possess the techniques to help him be so. What both government and industry needed, therefore, were new and effective methods for predicting and controlling costs. If incentive contracting were to be used more frequently, it was in fact essential that new methods be devised and used: because there would now be less leeway for error, new ways had to be found to reduce it.

One of these new methods was introduced by McNamara in 1962. It was called the "program definition phase" (PDP) technique; PDP represented an attempt to protect the government from committing large amounts of money to a program before it was fully defined.* It would do so by forcing the prospective contractors to do just that — to define as fully as possible the project that he was going to undertake, the difficulties that he expected to meet, the methods that he planned to use to solve them, and the amount of money that his solutions would cost. Too often in the past a contractor's proposals had been prepared in extreme haste, under severe competitive conditions, with costs hastily estimated and the promises of technological achievements vastly exaggerated.[11] Because the contractor did not clearly define his tasks *before* he began his development program, the government had to pay for errors that could have been avoided by preplanning *after* the development program was under way. Thus PDP was an attempt to remove as much of the uncertainty about the development program as possible before the program was begun. Its aims were:

> . . . the establishment of firm and realistic specifications, close definition of interfaces and responsibilities, identification of high risk areas, selection of the best technical approaches, and establishment of firm, realistic schedule and cost estimates.[12]

In effect, PDP was "contracted planning." Hereafter all development programs costing more than $25 million would be carried

---

* PDP was later called CDP — Contractor Definition Phase. The name changed but the process remained essentially the same.

out in two steps. Phase I would be the program definition phase; Phase II, the actual development of the weapon system. Defense companies would be selected for program definition contracts, not on the basis of detailed designs, but rather according to their ability to prove their competence to undertake and manage the contemplated program. (The government would award at least two FFP contracts for the program definition phase in order to preserve competition.) Since they were to be study contracts, and were not meant for the actual development, the FFP contract could last only about six months.[13] In order to ensure that the project would in fact be defined during Phase I, the output of these study contracts would be a series of planning documents that would detail the contractor's technical, management, and cost proposals for Phase II of his program. Contracts for Phase II would then be negotiated on the basis of these documents.

The PDP technique was designed to yield more reliable and hence more realistic estimates about the cost, time, and quality variables of the developmental process. It was based on two facts: (1) uncertainty declined (or estimates improved) as the developmental process proceeded, and (2) costs increased as development advanced. PDP would therefore come at the stage of the development cycle where the uncertainties were at their greatest, but where the costs of reducing them were at their lowest. In other words, the PDP technique would be economical: significantly improved estimates could be obtained at relatively low costs (with respect to total program costs).[14]

These two facts suggested still another to McNamara: following his cost-effectiveness approach, it would be both rational and economical to conduct at least two program definition efforts at the same time. Since the uncertainties were at a maximum in the earliest stages of the development cycle, it was not possible to predict with certainty whether one company's approach would work satisfactorily or at all. Only more knowledge, which the PDP technique was designed to produce, could answer these questions. Because time was crucial in the weapons race, however, the government could not take the risk of pursuing only one approach and then finding out that it was not feasible. Because the investment was relatively small to serve as a hedge against failures, it would be economical to pursue more than one approach.* The output of military hardware would justify the input of more human and material resources. It would be rational to maximize the alternatives at the early stages of development because there the uncertainties were highest and the costs lowest.[15]

The PDP technique would thus yield more knowledge. The government would benefit by being better able to weigh the trade-offs among the cost, time, and quality variables within one contractor's approach and among several. The defense contractor would benefit by obtaining the reliable estimates that he would need in assuming the greater risks of the incentive contract. If by the incentive contract the government would be forcing the contractor to assume more of the financial risks of development than he had to in the past, then with the PDP technique it would at least be giving him the chance to reduce the cost of these risks by paying him to study them more carefully.

McNamara obviously felt that the results that the PDP technique promised to yield justified its use. For the third phase in the evolution of the TFX — the runoff from January through November of 1962 — was in essence a program definition exercise. Three separate study contracts were given to each of the two competitors. By refusing to accept their cost estimates as realistic, McNamara forced the two competitors to think through their programs more fully. He wanted more documentation and analysis of their bids (as did the Navy). By having two approaches instead of one under

* How many approaches should in fact be pursued would depend on the importance of the program, the uncertainties surrounding it, and the costs of pursuing each additional approach. Generally, if the ultimate use of the program were judged to be of great value and if the uncertainties surrounding it were many, the costs of several approaches, even if they were high, would probably be justified.

study, he realized the benefits of parallel R & D efforts. He took advantage of the competitive atmosphere to help speed up and improve their work. If the TFX was not the first instance in which McNamara used the PDP technique, it was certainly one of the first.

McNamara's Reasons for Using the Incentive Contracting and PDP Techniques. McNamara and his "whiz kids" devised many other methods of reducing the cost optimism prevalent in development programs. However, we have discussed here only the incentive contract and the PDP techniques because they were two of the most effective methods of combatting the two things that McNamara believed to be most responsible for producing optimistic cost estimates. (The proviso was, of course, that both these devices be used under competitive conditions.) One of these stemmed from the peculiar competitive pressures to which a bidding company was subject; the other derived both from the budgetary constraints under which the services had to operate and from the high performance standards that they set in their development programs. The first factor was the tendency of bidding companies to "buy into" a program; the second, the tendency of the military services to do so.

The competition for major new air weapon system contracts put tremendous pressure on a company to buy into a program; that is, to try to win the development contract by purposely underestimating its (the company's) development costs. This pressure to buy into a program was so strong because the competition for new air weapon procurement was restricted solely to the *development* contract. Once the system had been designed, developed, and tested, no formal competition was usually held for the production contract. The company that developed the weapon system almost always received the contract to produce it.* In fact, if the govern-

---

* Waks mentions that one of the people whom he interviewed had stated that of the 38 major air weapon programs he had been involved with since 1939, in only one instance did the developer not receive the first production

ment wanted to minimize the costs, keep the lead time as low as possible, and maximize the performance of the system, it had no real choice but to award the production contract to the developer of the weapon.[16] Once the government had awarded a development contract to a company, it had in effect given this company a monopoly on the weapon system. The government and the company became locked together in a monopsony-monopoly relationship.

This relationship would not be so relevant to the problem of cost optimism were it not for another fact: in 1962, the real profits on a weapon system program came not from the development phase, where the uncertainties were too great to make large profits possible, but rather from the production phase, where the contractor could take advantage of the decreasing costs resulting from large-scale assembly runs. Thus the only way to realize large profits on a weapon system program was to be able to produce the weapon.[17] Since that required that a company be the developer, the competition for the development contract was the key to profits and therefore was very intense. A company would try to buy into the profits of the production contract by underestimating the costs of developing the system. Because development contracts were of the CPFF type, however, the company would pay no profit penalty for its optimistically low estimates: the government would pay for all new and "unexpected" costs.

The incentive contract was designed to remedy this situation. With it McNamara hoped to counter the tendency of the bidder to buy into the production contract by making him more responsive to and responsible for the costs incurred during development. He wanted to make the contractor pay for his own optimism. Even the incentive contract, though, could not eliminate all cost optimism. For if the company sustained a loss on the development of the weapon system under an incentive contract, it could make up this

---

contract. See Norman Waks, "Selective Competition in New Air Weapon Procurement" (unpublished Ph.D. dissertation, Harvard Graduate School of Business Administration, 1961), Chap. 3, p. 9.

loss by raising its price for the production contract. Since the company would have an effective monopoly on the production of the weapon, the government would find itself in a rather weak bargaining position to resist this price rise when it came time to negotiate the production contract.* It was for this reason that McNamara emphasized so forcefully the importance of the PDP technique. With it he could force each bidder to present him with realistic estimates by delaying the award of the development contract until he did so. Thus with the incentive development contract and the PDP technique, McNamara hoped to reduce that amount of cost optimism that resulted from the tendency of contractors to buy into a program.

The second cause of cost optimism that McNamara was determined to eliminate was that stemming from the tendency of the military services to buy into a program. This tendency resulted from two factors: (1) the tight budgetary constraints under which the services had to operate in planning for their weapons programs; and (2) the high performance standards that they set for these programs. As a result of the first factor, the services were continually faced with a dilemma in planning for their future military requirements. They knew that funds were limited and that they could not possibly hope to obtain everything they desired. Yet at the same time the military necessity and consequent bias to plan for all possible contingencies put them under strong psychological pressure to demand everything. The only ways of escaping from this dilemma were either to obtain everything or not to

---

* When a company submitted its cost bid on a weapon development program, it included the projected costs for development, production, and maintenance. However, the production contract was signed only after the actual development phase was nearing completion or had been completed. When a company signed a development contract, it did not therefore sign the production contract at the same time. Its estimates for production at that time thus were not legally binding. The government has since tried to change this situation through a device known as Total Package Procurement (TPP). Under TPP the development and production contracts are signed at the same time; that is, before the development phase is initiated.

demand everything. Since the former was impossible, the services were forced to concede the latter. But although they refrained from demanding everything they wanted, the services tried to ensure that they obtained everything that they asked for. When it was a matter of procuring advanced new weapon systems, one way that the services found successful was to discourage the companies from submitting realistic cost estimates.[18] By presenting a program as costing less than they knew it would, the services thereby hoped to crowd more programs into their inadequate annual budgets. Once money had been spent on a particular program, the services could argue that more money would be wasted by curtailing the program than by committing the additional funds necessary to complete it. By purposely underestimating the cost of a program, the services hoped to obtain the initial support of the service secretaries, the Bureau of the Budget, and the congress. Such support would help increase the odds that the program would in fact be finished. This was the first way in which the services tried to buy their way into a new weapon system program.

The second way the services tried was a variation on the first. Rather than offer only low estimates of a program's cost, they also gave high estimates for its performance. They put the premium on an advance in the "state of the art" to make the program look doubly attractive. But since a company's optimism was usually responsive to those things the services chose to emphasize, the companies also tended to promise high performance.[19] As a result, because they were optimistic in their estimates of both development costs and operational performance, the companies were submitting proposals that called for large technological advances but that lacked the equally large sums of money necessary to produce these advances. Moreover, since many of these advances went far beyond what was militarily necessary for the weapon to perform its mission, the Defense Department, so McNamara reasoned, found itself trapped into spending more than it had planned to, or more than the output of the weapon system was worth to it, or both.[20]

Because they tried to buy into a program by encouraging the competing bidder to submit low cost estimates and high performance promises, the services reinforced the bidder's already strong propensity to underestimate his development costs. McNamara predicted that more extensive use of the incentive contract for development programs would make the company realize that the risks of cost optimism now far outweighed its benefits. He could thereby neutralize the encouragement toward optimistic estimates that the services gave to the bidder by forcing the bidder to pay for them. With the PDP technique, he would be able to exercise much more control over the quality of the weapon system that the services asked for.* He could thereby prevent the services from "overbuying" on quality.[21]

McNamara thus opposed the optimism in a bidder's estimate of his development costs on two grounds. First, he said that such optimistic estimates misled the government into spending more than it had bargained for. Second, he said that such estimates misled the government into misallocating resources because they forced it to make decisions based on incorrect assumptions. McNamara wanted to restore rationality to the procurement of development programs. He therefore made realism in estimates of development costs his goal. He reasoned that only in this way could he make the "best" development decision: the one that used the nation's scarce resources most efficiently and the one that yielded the most effective weapon system for its price. In this way he could achieve both economy and quality in developing and procuring new weapon systems. The one did not have to be sacrificed in order to obtain the other.

Finally, because he felt that the tendencies of both the bidding companies and the military services to buy into a development

---

* How successful these two techniques were or could be expected to be in combating cost optimism and promoting cost realism and reduction will not be considered here. It is important that *McNamara* thought incentive contracting and program definition would be successful.

program were in large part responsible for cost optimism, he devised two techniques for combating them. The incentive contract would force the bidder to pay for his own optimism. The PDP technique would compel both him and the services to define their respective programs more fully and carefully so as to enable McNamara and his assistants to evaluate them more rigorously. By attacking cost optimism with such effort, McNamara was ultimately asserting that the cost of a program was a legitimate, rational, and necessary consideration in making decisions about it. He was not thereby asserting the primacy of the cost factor, but rather restoring its seemingly forgotten, proper place.

Source Selection Determinism

If his emphasis on cost realism helps to explain why McNamara chose his criteria for making his final decision on the TFX, then the peculiar problem caused by the System Source Selection process helps to show why he did not use those of the military officers.* This problem was inherent in the process. It resulted from the difficulty of trying to provide the civilian service secretary with the military advice that was essential for him to make a sound development decision, while trying to make sure that that very advice did not remove his freedom to choose among the alternatives. The service secretary was the one the law authorized to make the procurement decision, but the System Source Selection procedure tended to make his authority more formal than real. It turned the service secretary into a rubber stamp by forcing him to approve automatically whatever the military hierarchy recommended to him. The process decided for him rather than providing advice to him. The problem was thus one of determinism in the System Source Selection procedure. This determinism resulted from these

---

* The criteria that both McNamara and the military officers used in making their respective decisions are set forth in Chapter Five.

two factors: (1) the type of review through which every proposed major development decision in the Air Force had to go; and (2) the method of evaluation by which the Source Selection Board judged a bidder's proposal.

Reviewing the Proposed Decision. The secretary of each military department ought to and must seek the advice of his principal military personnel. The primary difficulty with the Source Selection procedure, however, was that the way in which it formulated and presented the Air Force secretary with this advice just about made the decision for him.[22] The System Source Selection process was just that — a "source selection" process. It did not merely *evaluate* alternative sources; it also *selected* a source (a company) to develop the weapon system being considered. It thereby equated evaluation with selection. It was designed to select a source as quickly as possible in order to proceed with the actual development as soon as possible. Because the system was meant to cut the time from drawing board to operational delivery, the advisory function became secondary.

The System Source Selection process presented the Air Force secretary with advice in the form of a recommendation that had passed up through both the bureaucratic channels and the military chain of command that were involved with the proposed development decision. It was this method of reviewing the proposed decision — the passage up through these two channels — that removed the secretary's freedom of choice.[23] For, once the Source Selection Board had reviewed the findings of the Evaluation Group and made its recommendation, the passage up through the remaining steps in Source Selection had the effect of establishing the validity of that recommendation. Each successive checkpoint, from the using command to the chief of staff, reinforced its validity until by the time it reached the secretary, the recommendation had acquired the force of a decision. Because so many people were involved in this review, because so many of them were high-ranking military officers, and because the review was so comprehensive (or at least appeared to be), the Air Force secretary in practice found it difficult if not impossible to disagree with the recommendation.[24]

If he chose to disagree with the recommendation, he would be doing so with the full knowledge that it was he who was ignoring the expert advice of his principal military commanders. If he chose to send the recommendation back to the Source Selection Board for re-evaluation (beginning the entire review once again), he would be doing so with the full knowledge that it was he who was delaying the moment when the actual development of the weapon would begin — the very thing that the system was designed to prevent. In either case he would appear to be making an arbitrary change in a valid, sound, and effective procedure. The fact that an Air Force secretary was hesitant to put himself in this uncomfortable position was illustrated by the testimony of Air Force Chief of Staff Curtis Le May. He stated that in the twenty-three development decisions in which he had participated under the System Source Selection procedure, the secretary had never overruled any of the recommendations that had been presented to him.[25]

Evaluating the Bidder's Proposal. The method of reviewing the recommendation of the Source Selection Board thus established and reinforced the apparent *validity* of that recommendation. But in addition, the manner in which the Board evaluated and judged a bidder's proposal established and enhanced the apparent *objectivity* of its recommendation. The Board used a numerical scoring system in order to rate the various proposals before it. These sets of figures presented the secretary with what appeared to be a clear-cut choice. They did not give him a feeling for the strengths and weaknesses of each proposal because they did not set forth alternative ways of looking at it. It was both the form in which the proposals were evaluated and the form in which the evaluations were given to the secretary that virtually compelled him to accept the recommendation.

However, the method that the Board used to evaluate the proposals before it was not really objective in the sense that the preferences and values of the men involved could have no influence on the outcome. The numerical scoring system disguised the true subjectivity of the evaluation method.[26] This system could only compare objectively a feature that was *identical* in all the submitted proposals. For example, it could evaluate the propulsion unit of each bidder, then compare the propulsion units of all the bidders, and then chose the best unit by seeing which had received the highest score. The objectivity of the scoring system broke down when it had to compare *different* features. It could evaluate the propulsion unit of each bidder, then the degree of cost realism of each bidder, but it could not then proceed to compare the performance of the propulsion unit of *A* to the degree of cost realism of *B* by looking at *A*'s rating and *B*'s rating on their respective items. The system was not capable of comparing propulsion units to cost realism because they are incommensurable items. It would therefore make no sense to try to do so. The only thing the scoring system could do was to evaluate the total number of features of each proposal. It would remain objective if the same criteria were used to evaluate the same feature of every proposal.

Yet, in itself, an evaluation of all the features of each proposal would not help someone who had to ˌchoose among proposals. Some way of comparing and ranking all the features of each proposal with those of every other was necessary if a choice were to be made. One way of doing this would be to determine which proposal had scored highest on the largest number of features (assuming that all the proposals had an equal number of features). This one could then be selected as the best proposal submitted. This method, however, would be an effective guide to choice only if all the features were of equal importance. For an airplane, at least, this assumption is not valid. A radar system may be more important than a propulsion unit if the primary mission of the plane is to defend a fleet of ships from a surprise enemy air attack by means of missiles. But if the primary mission is to attack the enemy deep within his own territory, then speed and hence the propulsion unit may be more important.

In other words, the features of a plane will vary in value according to the function that it is intended to perform or that those in power want it to perform. With each plane, some judgment must be made about the relative order of importance of all the features. Once the order of priority of the features has been determined, the different bidder proposals can be compared in their entirety with each other. If a numerical scoring system is used, the judgments about degrees of importance will reflect themselves most easily in a *weighted* rating system. For example, a perfect score on all the features may total a thousand points. The radar system may be worth up to twenty, whereas the propulsion unit is allotted up to one hundred. The propulsion unit would therefore be judged to be worth five times as much as the radar system.*

---

* In the TFX case the evaluation method worked as follows. The Evaluation Group was divided into four areas: management, technical, logistics, and operational (including the Navy's evaluation of carrier compatibility). Each section proceeded to develop raw scores for both of the proposals submitted in the area that it focused on. It did so by subdividing its area into individual items (or what it called "features"). For example, for the operational area, an item would be something like a propulsion unit or a radar system. The number of items within each area depended upon how the evaluators defined their respective areas. For example, the propulsion unit could be broken down into the engine and the air scoops (the air intakes for the engine). Both the engine and the air scoops could be considered features if they were so defined. Or the entire propulsion unit including these two could be defined as one feature. Each item within an area was rated by a scoring system going from zero to ten. The latter was the highest possible score an item could receive. Each item was given a raw score by comparing it to standards that the Source Selection Board had given to the Evaluation Group. Thus the proposals of the two competitors were not compared directly with each other, but with the same respective standards.

When the Evaluation Group had finished its work, it presented the Source Selection Board with raw scores that rated all the individual items of both competitors. The Board would then take the scores for each competitor, total them up within each area, and then multiply each of the four areas by some predetermined figure.

It was in this way that the Board weighted the raw scores. It put the scoring on a 1,000 possible-point basis (the perfect score). Of the 1,000 points, one-third was allotted to the technical area, one-third to the operational area, about one-fifth to the management area, and about one-ninth to the logistics area. From this weighted system it is clear that the Board felt performance (the operational area) was more important than

Judgments of this kind must be made if development proposals are to be evaluated and compared. These judgments, however, depend upon the values and preferences of the people who make them. A Navy officer would probably assign more importance to the radar system than to the propulsion unit. An Air Force officer might feel just the opposite. It is these value judgments — which are absolutely essential if the system is to work — that make the evaluation method subjective. By changing the order of priority of the features considered, different results can be obtained. A company that was first when propulsion units were valued at one hundred points might be last if they were valued at only ten. The evaluation method is therefore "loaded": the outcome can be determined by the manner in which the various features are weighted.

It was this weighted system of scoring that presented the Air Force secretary with a one-sided, distorted picture of the development proposals submitted. The Source Selection Board's recommendation seemed to be based on a relatively clear-cut, objective choice. But in reality, the secretary was being confronted with the biases and values of the military officers of the Board: it was they who weighted the features of the proposals. The Board did not offer him any alternative ways of looking at the proposals. He was given no idea of how the results might change if the weighting system were altered. The scoring system used by the Board thus forced the civilian secretary into judging its recommendation on the basis of the values and perspectives of the military officers. If he judged the proposals by his own criteria and reached different conclusions, the secretary would fall prey to being accused of arbitrariness.

Thus both the method of review and the manner of evaluation put the Air Force secretary into the position of presiding over rather than making decisions. Both these features of Source Selection reduced his initiative and restricted him in making development decisions. Both pressured the secretary to accept decisions

---

cost realism (the management area). These points will become much clearer in Chapter Five.

based on perspectives not necessarily coincident with his own. It was for all these reasons that McNamara refused to accept uncritically the four separate recommendations of the military hierarchy on the TFX. It was for all these reasons that he emphasized the factors he did because he knew that they were given minor weight in Source Selection. And it was for all these reasons that his decision looked all the more arbitrary and revolutionary. Because Source Selection engendered unanimous viewpoints among the military officers, his own decision — contrary to theirs — was put into that much sharper relief. Because the Air Force Source Selection process diluted civilian control over a development decision, McNamara was determined to alter it. Thereby he signaled his intention to strengthen the power of the civilian service secretary in these decisions.*

---

* There is direct proof of McNamara's dissatisfaction with the System Source Selection process. The Defense Industries Advisory Council (DIAC), formed in June of 1962, held its first meeting in the fall of that year to consider ways of changing Source Selection so as to give the civilian secretary more control over Air Force development programs. For a view of the changes then under consideration, see *Report of the DIAC*, in *TFX Hearings*, Vol. 5, pp. 1299–1300 and 1321–31.

The F-111B (foreground) and the F-111A, at the Fort Worth Division of the General Dynamics Corporation, prime contractor for the F-111 program.

FIVE · THE TFX CASE: PERFORMANCE, COST, AND COMMONALITY

The TFX was potentially the largest procurement contract that McNamara had awarded since becoming secretary of Defense in 1961. It was also the first major development program initiated by him. The TFX is therefore a good example to use in studying McNamara's new methods of making development decisions. All the elements of his innovating approach described in Chapter Four — the determination to obtain realistic cost estimates, the intention to make decisions as rationally as possible, the resolve to strengthen the power of the high-ranking civilian in Air Force development programs, and the aim to demonstrate the validity of the latter's institutional perspectives — all were evident throughout the history of the TFX. But they probably stand forth most conspicuously in the last decision affecting the TFX (the last decision, that is, before the contract was let and actual development was begun). For it is here, in the final decision of November, 1962 — the one in which McNamara awarded the contract to the General Dynamics-Grumman team — that the public record is most extensive.

111

The Evaluation

The easiest and most beneficial way of analyzing McNamara's decision is to do what McNamara himself did in evaluating the proposals of the two competitors. And that is to compare the two proposals in these three areas: (1) the operational performance each offered, (2) the realism of the cost estimates of each, and (3) the degree of commonality of each design. Before we can do that, however, we must outline briefly the scores that each competitor received in the fourth competition. These scores go a long way toward explaining why McNamara on the one hand and the military officers on the other took their respective positions.

The Fourth Competition Scores

In Table 5.1 are listed the scores that each competitor received in the fourth competition.* Out of a possible 1,000 points (a perfect score), the Boeing Company received 654.2; the General Dynamics-Grumman team, 662.4. In the four areas in which the competitors were judged, the greatest difference appeared in the operational area, where Boeing compiled 22 points more than its competitor. The smallest difference was in the logistics area, being less than 2 points. In both the management (cost) and technical areas, General Dynamics-Grumman received a rating superior to

TABLE 5.1. *Fourth Evaluation Scores*[a]

Area	Boeing	General Dynamics-Grumman	Perfect score
Technical	192.4	209.3	333.3
Operational	237.4	215.2	333.3
Management	135.3	150.2	222.2
Logistics	89.1	87.7	111.2
Total	654.2	662.4	1,000.0

[a] These are the weighted scores developed by the Source Selection Board.
Source: TFX Hearings, Vol. 9, p. 2519.

* See Chapter Four, pp. 106–107, for a detailed account of the scoring system employed by the Source Selection Board.

that of Boeing by 15 and 17 points, respectively. Of the four fields, then, each competitor scored better in two; but the General Dynamics-Grumman team had scored *substantially* better in two, whereas Boeing had done so only in one. The Boeing Company made up its relatively poorer performance in the technical and management areas by achieving a comparatively large lead in the performance area. This fact had a significance that will be discussed shortly.

Another important conclusion emerges from this table: the two total scores were very close. On the basis of the 1,000 point weighted system used by the Source Selection Board, the difference between the two totals was eight points or only eight-tenths of one per cent. This situation was a result of the three previous competitions. For in each instance the Evaluation Group had pointed out his respective deficiencies and mistakes to each competitor and both had gone back to work again to try to correct them. If all his deficiencies were pointed out often enough and if he were given enough time to correct them, each competitor would eventually solve the problems that the services' standards had presented to him. After a certain point in time, each competitor would therefore have reached a position about equal to that of the other: both would have solved the same problems, though they might have done so in different ways.[1] This is exactly what happened by the end of the fourth competition. In the first and second competitions the weighted scores had given the advantage to Boeing.[2] But by the end of the fourth, the General Dynamics-Grumman team had closed the gap with and even scored eight points better than Boeing.*

* There were no scores — raw or weighted — for the third competition. It was much too brief to allow the Evaluation Group to compile the raw scores that were necessary for the Source Selection Board to develop its weighted scores. Unfortunately, the *TFX Hearings* do not provide the weighted scores for the first two evaluations. It is therefore not possible to judge either how much better Boeing had done or how much of a gap the General Dynamics-Grumman team had closed. From the *Hearings,* however, it is known that in the first three rounds General Dynamics-Grumman

The Evaluation

This fact — that the final scores of the two competitors were so close as to be almost identical — raises serious questions about the efficacy of the weighted scoring system as a guide to choice in the TFX case. The system obviously works best when there is a substantial spread in the scores: the larger the difference, the greater the indication that the proposal with the higher score is probably the better one. This conclusion would be valid regardless of the criteria determining which was "better," as long as they were applied equally in judging each proposal. In the latter sense the system can be said to be the most "objective." It yields a relatively clear-cut choice, once the criteria of judgment and the particular formula for weighting these criteria have been accepted. As the scores move closer together, however, the effectiveness of the system as a guide to choice decreases. The smaller the spread in the scores, the less clear-cut the choice becomes.[3] The weighted scoring system loses almost all its effectiveness when it is applied to cases like that of the TFX: nearly identical scores preclude the possibility of any clear-cut choice. Eight-tenths of one per cent hardly seems a valid basis upon which to make a $7 billion decision. The weighted scoring system is subjective to begin with, by the very fact that it is weighted. Close scores like those in the TFX case make the system in addition arbitrary. "Military judgment" must now not only decide the criteria upon which to evaluate proposals and determine the manner in which these criteria are to be weighted. It must also "feel" its way to a decision when the weighted criteria fail to point the way to one. In cases like that of the TFX, the choice can almost be said to be one of "double military judgment."

This context is the only one in which the TFX decision can be understood. It is the only one in which the positions of the mili-

---

scored consistently higher than Boeing in the technical area. General Dynamics-Grumman was thus not behind Boeing in all areas and the latter had its chance to catch up in the technical area during these three rounds. See the testimony of Secretary of the Air Force Zuckert, Vol. 8, p. 1975.

tary officers on the one hand and McNamara and his civilian secretaries on the other can make any sense. Both the raw scores of
the Evaluation Group and the weighted scores of the Source
Selection Board merely confirmed the fact that the two proposals
were, for all practical purposes, equal. The final decision therefore had to be one of *judgment* because it was so close. Even the
military officers who opposed McNamara's decision admitted this
fact, as the following passage illustrates:

> SENATOR JAVITS. Would you say, therefore, that the issue before
> Secretary [McNamara] in choosing which of these two planes he
> would take was a mattter of judgment . . . ?
> GENERAL BENNETT. A matter of judgment, yes sir.
> SENATOR JAVITS. Do you consider that judgment so open and
> shut that you would say the Secretary was completely wrong
> about his choice?
> GENERAL BENNETT. No sir; I don't think it can be black or
> white to that extent.[4]

The judgments that each group made were necessarily based
upon and had to take account of its institutional perspectives and
responsibilities. Because the perspectives were different, so were
the judgments. Ultimately, therefore, the TFX decision did not
turn on who was right or wrong on the technical issues. Rather it
turned on the group that had the greater power to make *its* judgment on those issues prevail. It is now time to look at these
judgments.

Performance: Requirements vs. Extras

The Judgment of the Military Officers. After a thorough analysis
of each design, the Evaluation Group had concluded that:

> (1) Both contractors have the capability to successfully design
> and produce this weapon system.
> (2) Both designs are acceptable as initial development design
> configurations to the using agencies involved — TAC and the
> Navy. . . .

115

(3) When fully developed, the operational tactical aircraft will markedly improve the capability of the Tactical Air Command in carrying out its assigned missions, especially in limited war.

(4) Similarly, the Navy version, when fully developed and when configured with the new long-range, air-to-air missile, will markedly improve existing fleet air defense capability.[5]

The Evaluation Group had thus found that after almost a year of work, both companies finally met the performance standards that the Air Force and the Navy had set for them.

Nevertheless, although the Evaluation Group had found either design acceptable, the military officers found the Boeing design preferable. That this was so was primarily because of Air Force preferences, not those of the Navy. In the fourth competition the Navy had conducted an extensive evaluation of all aspects of each proposal, not, as it had done in the first three, of those aspects which pertained only to the carrier suitability of the designs. The body responsible for conducting the Navy's evaluation, the Bureau of Naval Weapons, had reported its conclusion on October 15 to the Source Selection Board:

> Overall, both designs are now considered acceptable. The level of carrier suitability and mission performance favors Boeing as in the previous submittals, but General Dynamics is now acceptable. The structural design approach used by General Dynamics is superior to that of Boeing. *There is no significant preference between the Navy versions of the two designs as submitted.*[6]

In the briefing presented to the Source Selection Board on November 2 by the Evaluation Group, the Navy cochairman, Captain Shepherd, restated this conclusion:

> There is no significant preference between the Navy versions of the two designs as submitted. . . . *On the basis of the proposals as submitted, there is no clear-cut choice between contractors.*[7]

Neither the Bureau of Naval Weapons nor Captain Shepherd, however, had the authority or the responsibility to make the Navy's formal recommendation. This right belonged to Admiral

Ashworth, the Navy's voting member on the Source Selection Board. He agreed with the other members of the Board, all Air Force officers, to recommend Boeing. Oddly enough, however, Ashworth was assistant chief for Research, Development, Test, and Evaluation of the Bureau of Naval Weapons, the very body that had reported only two weeks before that the Navy had no preference. In listing the reasons for his choice, Ashworth said one of the factors that persuaded him to select Boeing over General Dynamics-Grumman was "the substantial operational advantages" that the former's design promised to the Air Force.* In other words, precisely because either design was acceptable to it and precisely because it had no official preference, the Navy (and Admiral Ashworth) could afford to choose either design. In the opinion of the Bureau of Naval Weapons neither would be any more injurious nor any less advantageous to its interests than the other. Because the Air Force favored Boeing's design, the Navy agreed to go along with this choice.

If the Navy had no official preference (though, as we shall see, its officers had a *personal* one), the Air Force most emphatically did have one. General Sweeney, commander of TAC, expressed the Air Force point of view:

> There may be little to choose from between the two proposals as far as the Navy role is concerned. However, in my opinion

* Admiral Ashworth listed six other reasons for his choice that dealt with the supposedly superior operational performance that the Boeing design offered to the Navy:

(1) The Boeing design had a greater growth potential in carrier recovery characteristics.

(2) It had a lower gross weight.

(3) It had better subsonic flight operational characteristics so important for aircraft carrier operations.

(4) It performed the Navy's combat missions better.

(5) The Navy missile installation was better.

(6) It was cheaper both on the basis of the fixed-price bid, and the estimated cost based on Air Force standard cost experience.

One of these, the lower gross weight, will be discussed shortly. See Ashworth's prepared statement, *TFX Hearings,* Vol. 3, p. 665.

there is considerable difference between the two proposals as far as the TAC role is concerned. I believe that company X [the code letter for Boeing] has a much better aircraft with . . . advantages which make it far superior for the TAC role. . . .

I firmly believe that company X's proposal will produce a superior system that will provide a substantial improvement in the TAC capabilities. I believe just as firmly that company Y's [the code letter for General Dynamics] proposal will not provide the same increased capabilities.[8]

General Le May, Air Force chief of staff, spoke in the same vein:

The basis of my recommendation was my judgment that the operational advantages of the Boeing proposal outweighed the other factors involved.[9]

All the Air Force officers involved in the selection process preferred that Boeing develop the TFX because, in their judgment, certain features of Boeing's design did offer on paper to yield an airplane with performance superior to that of the General Dynamics-Grumman plane.* This fact was of the utmost importance and appeal to the Air Force. Under pressure from McNamara, the Air Force had reluctantly agreed to enter into a joint fighter program with the Navy. But in the ensuing attempt to draw up

---

* General Le May's and the other Air Force officers' preference for the Boeing design is somewhat puzzling. Though this proposal did offer certain features that appealed to the Air Force because they appeared likely to yield desirable operational characteristics, this same proposal did not meet the service's supersonic on-the-deck dash requirement. For the high-low-high interdiction mission — the one the Air Force considered primary — this dash performance was a necessity. Without it the airplane would offer little more than other, existing supersonic aircraft. The TFX was to be the first operational aircraft capable of *sustained* supersonic speeds on the deck. Though there were other aircraft that could attain such speeds on the deck, they could do so for only a few minutes before their fuel would be either very low or else exhausted.

The General Dynamics-Grumman proposal, on the other hand, did meet the Air Force's supersonic on-the-deck dash requirement. In view of these facts General Le May's and the Air Force's preference for Boeing — based on the extras to be discussed — seems again to emphasize that they were looking at what this company was promising to give them, rather than at the costs or reasonable likelihood of their doing so.

common performance standards, the Air Force found it had had to compromise on the specifications for those features that it wanted to have built into its next follow-on fighter. Because of the need to meet the Navy's requirements, the Air Force had had to accept a lighter, slower, smaller, and generally less versatile plane than it could probably have asked for, had it been able to develop on its own a TFX designed especially for its use. Finding itself in this situation, the Air Force would naturally favor the Boeing design: the superior features that it offered might enable the Air Force to obtain a plane that would come close to or even meet its original, uncompromised specifications (those it had drawn up in 1959–60). Since either plane satisfied the Navy, why should the Air Force not choose the one that promised to give the better performance for its missions? If both met the bi-service requirements, why not choose the one that offered to better these requirements? In short, why not choose the design with the "extras"? The Air Force did just that.

Many of these features or extras on the Boeing plane appealed to the Air Force (which the Boeing Company probably designed with the needs of that service paramount in its mind). Two of these, however, stood out and for this reason: they appeared most likely to provide the Air Force with a TFX more capable (than that of its competitor) of performing missions that the service felt were essential if this tactical fighter were to be of maximum use for the 1960's and 1970's. These two features or extras were: (1) thrust reversers and (2) top-mounted air inlets or "air scoops."

The supersonic jet fighter aircraft requires methods of braking for landings that its propeller-driven counterpart does not need. The latter uses wing flaps to reduce its air speed before it touches down on the runway and then reverses its thrust by changing the pitch of its propellers in order to help brake itself once it is on the runway. The supersonic aircraft, because it travels at higher speeds, needs more braking power when it is in the air than wing flaps alone can provide. Therefore it has also used what are called "spoilers" and "speed brakes" for landings. The former are per-forated sheets of metal that rise out from and perpendicular to the wing in order to increase the air friction and hence help re-duce the plane's air speed. The latter is a large, flat piece of metal that opens down from the belly of the fuselage to perform the same function. Once a supersonic aircraft is on the runway, it obviously cannot cause its jet engines to reverse the direction of their thrust in the manner in which the propeller-driven plane can do by reversing the pitch of its propellers. It must therefore resort to different methods to slow itself down once it is on the runway. One of the standard methods has been the use of the drag para-chute.

The General Dynamics-Grumman team proposed to use these three experience-tested and proven devices — spoilers, speed brakes, and drag parachutes — to brake the TFX before and after land-ing. The Boeing Company, however, proposed to use one device to take the place of these three: the thrust reverser. This was a metal apparatus that would be attached to the rear of the engine and that would deflect the exhaust gases forward (in the direction in which the plane would be flying) instead of allowing them to shoot backward (in the direction away from which the plane would be flying).[10] The thrust reverser would thereby do what its name implied: it would reverse the thrust of the engine and con-sequently reduce the speed of the aircraft. By so braking the plane, the thrust reverser would have the same effect as the re-versing of the propellers had on the propeller-driven plane.

The thrust reverser, though it had been used on commercial jet transports for landings, had been used very little, if at all (as of 1962), on combat aircraft.[11] Nevertheless, it did promise to pro-vide greater braking power for landings than both spoilers and drag chutes combined could give. This was the first important characteristic of the thrust reverser: by offering more braking power, it would enable the TFX to reduce its speed more quickly, stop more quickly, and require a shorter distance for landing.

120

However, since an airplane can land in a distance shorter than it requires for takeoff, this additional braking power was not crucial for landings. Though it would allow the TFX to stop in a shorter distance upon landing, the thrust reverser would not reduce the length of the runway required for operating the plane. For that was determined by the length of the runway the plane required for takeoff, not that which it required for landing.

Thus it was the second characteristic of the thrust reverser that was really important to the Air Force: it could be used during the in-flight maneuvering of the plane. The Boeing Company proposed to improve the performance of the TFX by employing the thrust reverser in all phases of the plane's flight. It would make use of the deflecting powers of this device to increase the in-flight maneuverability of the TFX by permitting steeper angles of descent than would otherwise be possible.* This promised increase in the in-flight performance of the TFX naturally appealed to the Air Force. The better its operation in the air, the greater would be its chances of destroying any enemy aircraft that it might encounter and hence the greater the odds that it could successfully complete its interdiction and air superiority missions. By using thrust reversers instead of spoilers and drag chutes, the Boeing Company held an appealing vision before the eyes of a receptive Air Force (one that its competitor failed to arouse): a TFX with improved performance. The Air Force chose accordingly.

The second extra that appealed to the Air Force was Boeing's use of top-mounted air scoops. Air scoops are the inlets or intakes that channel air (oxygen) into the compressor of the jet engine. Their position on the plane can affect the performance of the engine. The General Dynamics-Grumman team proposed to place the air scoops under the wing at the point where the wing met the fuselage. The advantage of placing them there lay in the fact that

---

* The problem with steep angles of descent is that they are hard to pull out of. By slowing the aircraft when it is in such descents, the thrust reverser makes it easier to pull out of them.

airplane manufacturers had had a great deal of experience with air scoops in this position and could make the air scoops rather efficient (in engine combustion) if they were placed there.[12] For the TFX, however, this under-the-wing position had two potential disadvantages: the possibility of foreign-object-ingestion damage and the possibility of flameouts. First, because these scoops were under the wing and behind the nose wheels, there was the real danger that they would ingest the debris kicked up by these wheels during takeoffs and landings. If any of this debris (twigs, gravel, or pebbles) were ingested by the scoops, it would then enter the engine and most probably damage the compressor blades or the turbine blades.[13] That would disable or even destroy the engine.

If the first possibility — foreign object ingestion — could destroy the engine, the second — flameouts — could cause it to cease functioning temporarily. If the scoops were under the wing, they might be next to or very near missiles. The blast from the ignition of these missiles could cause the engine to flameout — to quit firing by disturbing the even flow of air into the air scoops.[14] In order to prevent flameouts, the missiles would have to be placed far enough away from the air scoops that their ignition could have no injurious effect on the even flow of air to the engine. This consideration, because it required some distance between the scoop and the missile, limited the number of missiles that the TFX could carry on its wings.

The Air Force cared for neither potential disadvantage inherent in the General Dynamics-Grumman design. Both threatened to lower its effectiveness, though in different ways. One of the really new advantages that the TFX was to embody would be its ability to operate from clandestine, austere, makeshift airfields. On these types of fields the amount of debris and hence the possibility of foreign-object-ingestion damage would be much greater than if the TFX were operating from concrete, permanent, known airstrips. The Air Force felt that the under-the-wing position of the air scoops did not provide sufficient protection against debris ingestion, even with deflectors behind the wheels and in front of the air scoops. With the General Dynamics-Grumman design, the Air Force saw the deployment flexibility of the TFX endangered. Second, because of the need to provide for the possibility of flameouts, the armament load and the weapon-carrying versatility of the TFX would be reduced. Both of these reductions might seriously endanger the close-support mission of the TFX.

On the other hand, the Boeing design appeared to the Air Force to contain neither of these disadvantages. With air scoops mounted on top of the fuselage and away from debris and missiles, the possibility of both debris ingestion and flameout were reduced to a minimum.[15] The position of Boeing's air scoops did not threaten to lessen the TFX's deployment flexibility, nor did it place any limitations on its armament carrying ability. The Air Force chose accordingly.

A third feature in the Boeing design made the Navy's officers, though their Bureau of Naval Weapons had officially found that either design would meet its requirements, personally favor the Boeing proposal. This feature, together with the Air Force preference for Boeing, helped to persuade Admiral Ashworth to vote with the Air Force officers on the Source Selection Board. This feature was Boeing's proposed use of titanium for the wing carry-through structure. This structure was the part of the wing that contained the pivot joint on which the wings would sweep either forward or backward (see Figure 5.1). This structure would have to bear up under a great deal of stress because it was the point of attachment of the wings to the fuselage. The General Dynamics-Grumman team proposed to use steel and aluminum for this structure; the Boeing Company, titanium.[16] In either instance, the structure would have to be rather thick to compensate for the stresses to which it would be subjected. The thicknesses required meant in turn that more weight would have to be added to the plane. Weight is always a critical factor in any plane, but it was especially so to the TFX as the Navy envisioned it. For this service wanted it to

123

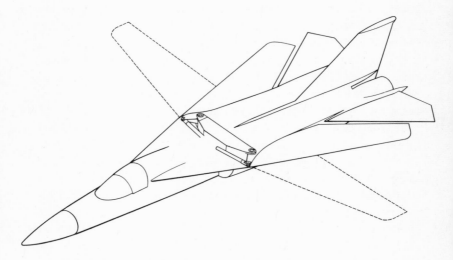

FIGURE 5.1. *The wing carry-through structure of the F-111*

have as great a loiter capability as was possible for its fleet air defense mission. With a given fuel-tank capacity, the lighter the TFX,
the longer it could fly. Titanium is approximately one-half as
heavy as steel.[17] Therefore, by using this metal in the wing carry-
through structure (and in other stress areas of the plane), Boeing
offered to the Navy a plane lighter than the one its competitor
offered. A lighter plane would not only increase the distance and
time that the plane could loiter above the fleet, but also would
give the Navy an aircraft more compatible with carriers and with
greater growth potential. The Navy chose accordingly.

These three features — thrust reversers, top-mounted air scoops,
and titanium wing carry-through structures — probably made the
Boeing plane, on paper at least, appear to the Air Force and Navy
officers to be superior to that of the General Dynamics-Grumman
team. They offered to improve the in-flight performance of the
plane above what was required. They promised to reduce the like-

124

lihood that it would be caught on the ground in a surprise enemy air attack. They appeared to lengthen the time and miles that the plane could fly. In short, they seemed to make the TFX better able to perform TAC's three missions of interdiction, air superiority, and close support, while enabling the Navy to perform its fleet air defense mission more effectively. It is no wonder, then, that the Air Force and Navy officers picked the Boeing design even when they were told by their technical experts that both had met the performance standards. Boeing's design appeared to them to go much further beyond these standards. That was what they wanted.

The Judgment of the Civilian Secretaries. It was for precisely the same reasons that the military officers picked the Boeing design that McNamara and his civilian secretaries — Korth, Zuckert, and Gilpatric — did not. The same features that made the Boeing design attractive to the Air Force and Navy officers made it unattractive to the civilian secretaries. The same Boeing features that the Air Force and Navy officers saw as promising "extra" performance, McNamara and his advisers saw as promising "extra" development risks. McNamara was very critical of what he considered to be the services' strong tendency to overbuy on performance quality in their weapon systems by setting standards that went far beyond meeting the essential military requirements.[18] He saw this tendency to overbuy prevalent in the two services' decisions on the TFX. He said:

> . . . the Source Selection Board, using factors weighted by judgment, made a recommendation which appeared to place greater emphasis on potential bonus factors in certain operational areas, rather than on dependability of development and predictability of costs. This recommendation, understandably, was seconded by the Navy and Air Staffs, since these officers are most vitally interested in obtaining the ultimate in performance in individual weapon systems.[19]

Secretary of the Air Force Zuckert expressed the same opinion:

> You are talking here with operational people who have held
> out to them the prospect of certain advantages which appeal to
> them. I don't think they had a balanced view of the technical
> difficulties.[20]

McNamara and Zuckert, in effect, assumed two things: (1) the
judgments of the military officers were necessarily biased and narrow because of their institutional and professional perspectives;
and (2) their own judgments were necessarily broader because of
the biases that their institutional and lay perspectives gave rise to.
It was the military officers who had to develop the war plans to
provide for all possible contingencies. It was they who were responsible by rank and position to see that their services had
weapons better than those of the enemy. It was they who were
responsible for and mindful of the lives that would be saved or
lost depending on the quality of the weapons they provided. It
was they who had to push for those "extras," because no one else
would. Because of all these factors, the extras began to look like
essentials to the military officers. As an Air Force general once
said: "A second-best airplane is like a second-best poker hand.
No damn good."[21]

On the other hand, the civilian secretaries, though they were
mindful of all these factors, saw others that put the concerns of
the military officers in a slightly different, if not less important,
light. It was they who had to be mindful of the overall size of the
national defense effort. It was they who had to maintain the balance among the parts of that program. It was they who had to
consider the effects that the costs of one service program might
have on the possibilities of the other services' programs. And with
the advent of McNamara, it was they who tried to measure the
amounts of military effectiveness that respective outlays would
purchase. (In effect, McNamara also wanted the military to consider the costs of a program as relevant for making decisions about
it as they judged its potential military usefulness to be.)

To Korth, Zuckert, Gilpatric, and McNamara, the performance

extras that Boeing proposed increased the development risks in time, quality, and costs. As Secretary Zuckert said:

> Again and again, the Air Force engineers warned that innovations in the Boeing design created serious technical problems, and might not work out as predicted by the contractor. Granted that Boeing might solve these problems, the risk was that, in the process, the performance of the TFX might be degraded, its delivery to our tactical forces delayed, and its costs increased by millions, perhaps hundreds of millions.[22]

They were mindful of the fact that the quality of a given weapon system increases only with an increase in cost and a delay in the date of operational delivery. Moreover, they were aware that additional increments of quality in a weapon system became increasingly (or proportionately) more expensive in development time and costs. Each additional unit of money and time would buy a correspondingly smaller unit of quality improvement. They believed the variable-sweep wing to be a large enough development risk in itself. Why complicate the development process by "cumulating" the risk, that is, by adding extras that would themselves require much effort to develop.[23] Why choose the approach of Boeing, which exceeded the required performance specifications, but which also increased the risk, when the more straightforward approach of the General Dynamics-Grumman team would meet the specifications and avoid the increase in risk? In short, why choose the technically more risky design when both met the performance standards?

It was thus McNamara's and his advisers' argument that the Boeing design included features that seriously complicated the development effort, but were not essential to the realization of the basic military requirements as the two services themselves had defined them. Their analysis of each of the three features that had appealed to the Air Force and Navy illustrates their line of argument. First, with respect to thrust reversers, the civilian secretaries pointed out that they had never been used in flight on an operational fighter aircraft; nor had they ever been used on supersonic aircraft.[24] They said that the type of thrust reverser proposed by Boeing would have to function over the entire speed range of the TFX, from zero to mach 2.2, that the temperatures to which it would be subjected would approach 3,000°F., and that a loss of efficiency of 3 per cent in the thrust reverser (due to warpage or leaks) would decrease the supersonic dash capability of the TFX by 25 per cent. They stated that no known thrust reverser of this type existed, that those used in commercial planes functioned only at very low speeds for landing, and that the highest temperature to which they were subjected was 1,200°F.[25]

Moreover, McNamara pointed out that in addition to considerable wind-tunnel testing, extensive flight tests would have to be conducted in order to demonstrate that the thrust reverser worked and that it had no adverse effects on the longitudinal and directional stability of the plane. Flight testing, however, cannot come until very late in the development phase. If the device did not work as expected or proved to be unreliable, the operational delivery of the TFX would be much delayed; and the costs of development would be increased. Both would occur because Boeing had not provided for a deceleration mechanism to back up the thrust reverser.[26] The Boeing approach was "an all or nothing at all" application of a thrust reverser that had yet to be developed. Because its thrust reverser was an unknown, the civilian secretaries felt it contained too many risks to the program to justify its use.

On the other hand, the General Dynamics-Grumman design avoided all these problems because it had used the historically proven speed brake, spoiler, and drag-chute techniques. With this approach the team had exceeded the work statement requirements for in-flight and ground deceleration (though not as far as Boeing had with the thrust reverser). The choice between the two approaches was thus a question of judgment — a judgment of the trade-offs between a technically straightforward and operationally satisfactory approach versus an operationally superior but technically risky one. The civilian secretaries chose accordingly.

Second, after studying Boeing's top-mounted air scoops, the civilian secretaries pointed out that although this position minimized the possibilities of foreign-object-ingestion damage and flameouts, it nevertheless imposed performance limitations on the TFX. Because the scoops were on the fuselage, the boundary layer of air (the air closest to the skin of the fuselage) would encounter much resistance because of the friction caused by coming into contact with the fuselage skin. This resistance would slow this boundary air layer, causing it to enter the air inlet at a speed lower than that of those layers of air farther from the fuselage skin. The uneven speed of the air layers entering the air scoops would in turn significantly distort the airflow to the engine and result in a degradation of engine performance.[27] At high angles of attack (positions of descent that make the plane deviate sharply from a horizontal path) during supersonic flight, the airflow distortion would become prohibitive. The top-mounted air scoops therefore posed potential limits on and risks to the in-flight maneuverability of the TFX. Moreover, the effects of these limits would not and could not be known until extensive flight tests (which could be undertaken only in the late stages of development) were carried out.

On the other hand, the General Dynamics-Grumman team's under-the-wing position involved much less of an airflow distortion problem. Though this position did involve some danger of debris ingestion and flameouts, the secretaries pointed out that the Evaluation Group had concluded that a reasonable development effort would solve these problems.[28] Again the choice between the alternatives was a judgment of the trade-offs. The Boeing approach would solve the debris ingestion and flameout problems only at the expense of creating another, whose full effects could not be known until very late in development. The General Dynamics-Grumman approach could solve these two problems with a reasonable expenditure of effort and could do so without creating other problems. The civilian secretaries chose accordingly.

Third, after analyzing Boeing's use of titanium in the wing carry-through structure, the civilian secretaries pointed out that titanium had never been used in the major structural members of aircraft in the thickness that the Boeing design required (about one inch). As a result, the thickness called for exceeded the published guarantees of the titanium and aircraft industries.[29] Moreover, the Air Force had more experience with titanium than had Boeing. For in 1962, the Lockheed Aircraft Corporation was working on a mach 3 interceptor aircraft called the A-11. Its existence at that time was such a closely guarded secret that not only were Boeing, General Dynamics, and Grumman unaware of its existence, but so too were many Air Force officers. The A-11 had to make extensive use of titanium because of the high temperatures generated by mach 3 speeds. (Mach 2.5 is the upper limit for aluminum, because that metal has no sustained resistance to temperatures generated by higher speeds.) In November of 1962, Secretary Zuckert made a personal trip to Lockheed to talk to the engineer primarily responsible for designing and building the A-11 — Kelly Johnson. Johnson was one of the most respected men in aeronautical engineering in the United States and also one of the most experienced designers of supersonic aircraft in the world. Based on his experience with the A-11, Johnson told Zuckert that Boeing was "crazy" to use titanium in the thickness and places it was proposing to. Johnson said that Boeing was only complicating the development effort when it was not necessary to do so. He stated that because of the uncertainties and difficulties involved in such uses of titanium, the primary justification in the TFX case for using that metal should be for temperature considerations. Since the TFX could not go above mach 2.5, however, there was no need for such uses of titanium. Aluminum (and steel) would suffice. This confirmation from an outside expert experienced in the use of this metal thus reaffirmed the advice that Zuckert had received from his personal advisers.[30]

Finally, the secretaries referred to two conclusions of the Evaluation Group: (1) even though Boeing had had no experience with this thickness, the company had submitted no load or stress analysis for the use of titanium in the wing-pivot section; and (2) as a result, Boeing's wing-pivot mechanism failed to meet work statement requirements except at room temperatures.[31] Whether the use of this metal would be successful could not be known until late in development after extensive flight testing. If it were not successful, the consequences would be severe:

> Not only might the substitution of less exotic metals itself be likely to trigger a series of design changes; it would also impose weight and hence performance penalties, the correction of which would require major redesign efforts, impeded program progress, and greatly increase costs.[32]

On the other hand, the General Dynamics-Grumman team had proposed the use of two conventional, though heavier, metals — steel and aluminum — whose stress, fatigue, and thermal strengths were well known. Thus again a judgment about the trade-offs had to be made — this time between the weight-saving but risky Boeing approach versus the proven, heavier, but satisfactory, General Dynamics-Grumman approach. The civilian secretaries chose accordingly.

Thus each group — the military officers and the civilian secretaries — looked at the same proposals but saw different things. Because the military concentrated on quality in their weapon systems, they saw the Boeing design as the better one. Because the civilian secretaries had to consider the *cost* of quality as well as quality itself, they saw the Boeing design as the riskier one. The military judged that the increase in performance promised by the Boeing design made that design superior and therefore preferable. The civilians judged that the increase in performance promised by the Boeing design could be achieved only by increased expenditure and injurious delays. The extras that the military officers thought would bring a valuable improvement in operational quality, the civilian secretaries judged would bring an unacceptable increase in development risk.

Yet even though the judgment of each group was contrary to that of the other, both were nevertheless valid. That this was so was due primarily to the nature of the evaluation process in which each group participated. For this procedure was meant more to determine the probability that a contractor could and would do what he had promised to do, rather than to analyze and then evaluate what a contractor had done.[33] Each contractor had only put designs on paper, not flown planes in the sky. Each group was therefore judging the *proposals* of both contractors, not the *results* of their development efforts. But because the uncertainties are greater at the design stage than at the development stage, even the technical experts disagreed on both the probability and desirability of attaining the design promises. Because there could be no empirical proof at this stage in development to validate or invalidate either group's judgments, both remained valid. But because one group possessed the political power and statutory authority to enforce its will, its judgment on performance prevailed.

Cost: Realism vs. Optimism

In his July 13, 1962 letter to the two competitors for the TFX development contract, Deputy Secretary of Defense Gilpatric had listed the three key criteria according to which the companies would be judged and the winner selected.* These were: (1) satisfaction to the Navy and TAC that the winning design would add significantly to their respective tactical air capabilities; (2) "demonstrably credible understanding of costs"; and (3) "minimum divergence from a common design." With the conclusion of the fourth competition, McNamara found that both competitors had

* See Chapter Three, p. 76.

met the first criterion: each service judged that both designs would add significantly to its present capabilities. The disagreement between McNamara and the two services was not over whether both designs had met the performance specifications, but rather over which had done so with the least development risks. Having decided that this was most nearly true of the General Dynamics-Grumman design, McNamara proceeded to consider his second criterion.

The Bidders' Cost Estimates. In evaluating the fourth cost estimates of the two competitors, the management section of the Evaluation Group had reached two general conclusions:

(1) for cost realism, both contractors' estimates remain[ed] low;

(2) Boeing was estimated to be 21% low; General Dynamics 18% low.[34]

Thus, although both contractors were still optimistic in their estimates, Boeing was more so. The Source Selection Board had concurred in this conclusion, and it had given the General Dynamics-Grumman team a 15 point margin over its competitor in the management or cost area (150.2 to 135.3).

McNamara read the conclusions of these two bodies. He then analyzed each contractor's cost data and compared the data of the two. In performing this task, he could have used three different sets of figures. These figures are summarized in Table 5.2. The first set was the contractor's own bids, that is, the prices at which each proposed to contract for the TFX program. For the development phase (R & D), these figures were $466.6 million for Boeing and $543.5 million for General Dynamics-Grumman. For the total program (development and production), these figures were $5,364.3 million and $5,455.5 million, respectively. The second set of figures was the Air Force adjusted estimates. These were $576.8 and $711 million, respectively, for R & D and $5,387.5 and $5,803.5 million, respectively, for total program costs. These adjusted estimates were made because the contractors' own bids contained no estimates of the cost of engineering changes. Rather they included estimates only of the specific work that the contractors set forth in their design proposals. Because of the uncertainties and complexities inherent in development, however, engineering changes (alterations in the design) were very common and often involved rather large departures from the original plans. To allow for these changes, the Air Force evaluators made an estimate, based on the experience of similar past programs, of the costs that these changes in each design would entail, and then added them to the contractor's own proposals.[35] In this manner the contractors' proposals were adjusted to the higher Air Force estimates.

TABLE 5.2. *Summary of TFX Cost Estimates* (in millions of dollars)

	R & D		Total[a]	
	Boeing	*General Dynamics-Grumman*	*Boeing*	*General Dynamics-Grumman*
Contractor's proposal	466.6	543.5	5,364.3	5,455.5
Air Force adjusted estimates	576.8	711.0	5,387.5	5,803.5
Air Force estimating standards	873.0	918.0	6,983.0	7,083.0

a Includes R & D and production costs.
Source: TFX Hearings, Vol. 1, pp. 208–209.

The last set of figures was the Air Force estimating standards. These figures were $873 and $918 million, respectively, for R & D and $6,983 and $7,083 million, respectively, for total program costs. These Air Force standards represented the estimates of what the Air Force evaluators thought the TFX program *should* cost. They were made independently of and without reference to the contractors' own bids. (In fact these standards were developed by the Evaluation Group prior to receiving any contractor proposals in December, 1961.) What the evaluators did was to determine what all the elements necessary in a program to produce the TFX should be, and then on the basis of experience with other fighters, to project what the costs of these elements should be. For example, the evaluators calculated how many tooling hours (the time necessary to produce all the parts of the plane on the assembly line machines or tools) would be required for the TFX. Their estimate was 6.9 million hours. They then estimated the cost of these tooling hours. On the other hand, the Boeing Company in its bid calculated that it would require 3.9 million tooling hours; the General Dynamics-Grumman team estimated that it would need 7 million tooling hours.[36] The Air Force standards were thus based on a hypothetical TFX whose principal elements were completely unrelated to and not derived from the contractors' own figures.* These two standards — one for R & D and one for total program costs — were developed by the Air Force in order to give it some idea of how large the TFX program could be expected to be.

McNamara could have used any or all three of these sets of figures to compare the cost estimates of the two competitors. He chose to use none of them. It was his contention that none of these figures was reliable either for estimating the *difference* between the cost estimates of the two or therefore for *choosing* between them.[37] On the basis of the conclusions of the Evaluation Group and on the estimates made by his own advisers, McNamara concluded that the contractors' own bids were unreliable because they

---

* The discrepancies between the figures of the two competitors within each standard (R & D and total program costs) are due to the adjustments made by the evaluators to account for the General Dynamics-Grumman team's higher labor rates and greater overhead costs. The differences — $45 million for R & D (918–873) and $100 million for total program costs (7083–6983) — are relatively small when compared to the huge amounts involved.

Moreover, these differences in figures do not contradict the fact that the standards were developed independently of each contractor's own figures. For example, the same number of tooling hours — 6.9 million — were used for each proposal. In essence only two standards (for R & D and total program costs) were developed. After they were completed, small changes were made to allow for the differences in labor and overhead costs.

135

were much too optimistic. Because both competitors had offered estimates far below what he believed they should be and would prove to be, McNamara reasoned that it would make no sense for him to estimate the cost difference between the two bids by comparing them to each other. For that reason, the Air Force adjusted estimates were just as unreliable and just as useless: they incorporated into their figures the very same optimism as that of the bidders' own estimates.

Finally, the Air Force estimating standards were of no help in determining the difference in amount between the cost estimates of the two competitors. These estimates could serve only as a standard — a common denominator against which the two proposals could be tested for cost *realism* but not for actual cost *difference*.[38] Each bid could be compared to the standard in order to assess its cost realism or optimism, because the standard represented what the Air Force projected the actual size of the TFX program would be. Such a comparison would therefore give a rough indication of the contractor's understanding of the costs involved. To compare the two bids against the same standard, however, was not equivalent to measuring the difference in amount between them. This was so for two reasons. First, the optimism of the competitor's own bids would make such a measurement unreliable. But second and more important, such a measurement would be unreliable because it would be invalid: the two bids were incommensurable quantities. If each competitor were offering to produce exactly the same plane and to do so in exactly the same way, then the two cost estimates would be commensurable because they would represent estimates of like quantities. However, because the two planes were designed differently and because different engineering processes were going to be used to develop them, each competitor's cost bid represented an estimate of a quantity significantly different from the other's. Thus, though the cost estimates were expressed in comparable language — dollars — they were nevertheless estimates of incommensurable quantities. This fact in turn made a comparison of the cost estimates by reference to a third quantity invalid.[39] Therefore, although the Air Force standards could be used as a basis for roughly determining the cost realism of each of the two estimates, they could not be used as the basis for figuring the difference in amount between them.

McNamara concluded, moreover, that although these standards could be used to judge cost realism, they were nevertheless of limited value in doing so. He was skeptical about the ultimate worth of these standards for two reasons. First, experience with past programs (such as Skybolt — a long-distance surface-to-air missile that McNamara canceled when he saw the development costs becoming prohibitive) had shown that these standards were much too low. Second, he saw that only 1 per cent of all the working hours of the Evaluation Group (more than 270,000 man-hours) had been spent in evaluating the contractors' cost proposals. Only a small fraction of this 1 per cent had been used to draw up the estimating standards.[40] For both reasons McNamara concluded not only that these figures were unreliable for judging optimism, but also that "the Air Force simply did not have an adequate system for estimating total program costs."[41]

McNamara thus found himself in a rather difficult, if not highly uncomfortable, situation. From the Evaluation Group's conclusions, from his staff's analysis, and from his own rough estimates, he knew that both bids were too low. He also knew that one bid was lower than the other. But from none of the figures before him could he know *how* low the two bids were or how *much* lower one was than the other. Faced with this situation, unable to use any of the figures developed by the Air Force, not trusting those submitted by the contractors, how did McNamara arrive at his final conclusions with respect to costs? The following passage gives a clue:

> The Secretary said that, after finding the Air Force estimates inadequate for judging the cost implications of the two proposals,

he had made rough judgments of the kind he had made for many years with the Ford Motor Co.* It did not take very much time to do this because the technical differences between the proposals had rather obvious cost implications.[42]

In other words, what McNamara did was to concentrate on finding some way of estimating the costs that the different technical and design approaches of the two competitors would involve. He therefore tried to do what none of the figures had enabled him to do: to estimate the difference in cost inherent in the differences in the designs and engineering techniques of the two competitors.

---

* It is certainly fair to ask why McNamara relied *only* on what he called "rough judgment," rather than having his own staff prepare more detailed, rigorous analyses. From the public record and from the interviews I held, there seems to be no conclusive answer to this question. There are, however, several *possible* answers. First, McNamara may have felt he had all the information he needed to make a sound decision. In this case more detailed staff analysis would have been superfluous. Second, he may have felt that the information he would have gained by having his staff do such analysis would have been outweighed by the delay required for them to do so. In this case more detailed staff analysis would have been unjustifiable.

Neither of these answers seems to be the correct one. About the first, McNamara stated that neither the contractors' own estimates nor the Air Force's estimating standards were useful to him in projecting either the likely costs of the TFX development program or the difference in costs between the two competitors' programs. (The fact that the development program has run well over $1 billion suggests that he was correct.) It is hard to imagine that McNamara would therefore not have wanted something that could have provided him with more information than he had. With his predisposition for knowing the alternatives and with his known bent for rigorous analysis, it is hard to imagine McNamara relying upon "rough judgment" unless he felt he had been forced to do so. With regard to the second answer, McNamara had already delayed the awarding of the development contract ten months — from January to November — in order to get better estimates and designs. It is hard to imagine that McNamara would not have found justifiable those few extra weeks or even months that would have been required for a staff analysis if such an analysis might have produced some valuable information.

Thus the unlikelihood of either of these possibilities points to the same conclusion: McNamara probably felt that he was not going to receive any *more* useful cost data (useful in the sense that the data would help him make a choice between the two competitors) because he felt that he had not received *any* useful cost data as a result of the four rounds. He did not

In doing so, McNamara proceeded on the assumption that the Boeing design was the riskier because it promised to achieve the larger advances in technology. In turn, because it offered the superior performance, McNamara reasoned that the Boeing design would require larger cost outlays than its competitor's design: the extras would necessitate extensive development efforts and hence large costs in themselves.[43] Upon examining the Boeing Company's proposal, however, McNamara found that its cost estimates did not coincide with his expectations regarding them. For example, he found Boeing's estimates of the cost of thrust reversers to be incredibly optimistic. In its fourth proposal,

---

obtain it from the Air Force nor would he obtain it from his staff. For McNamara believed that neither he nor his staff nor the Air Force possessed at that time either the historical backlog of cost information or the statistical equations based on such a backlog to make more than "rough judgments" about the actual costs of major aircraft development programs.

In addition to the evidence from interviews I received for this hypothesis, there are two other shreds of information. The first is a short statement on the TFX case by a man who worked in the Defense Department while the key decisions were being made on the TFX, and who was very close to McNamara while there. In an article on McNamara's methods of running the Defense Department, Adam Yarmolinsky said: "It is an essential element of his management philosophy to reach out for decisions. But he could not find the factual background for decision making if the system did not dredge it up for him. A case in point was the decision to choose General Dynamics over Boeing as the contractor for the TFX. In order to evaluate properly the cost estimates submitted by the two final bidders, both of which were unreasonably optimistic, the Secretary would have needed a compilation of experience statistics based largely on so-called learning curves, which was simply not available at that early stage in his administration. Instead he had to base his decision on his own business experience." See "How the Pentagon Works," *The Atlantic Monthly,* CCXIX (March, 1967), 60–61.

A second bit of evidence lies in two of the steps that McNamara took to remedy the situation that Yarmolinsky describes above. Early in 1963, probably as a direct result of his experience with the TFX, McNamara instructed his office of Systems Analysis to produce some techniques that would enable him to estimate development costs for aircraft with greater accuracy than he could have in the TFX case. One result has been a series of estimating equations developed through multiple regression analysis that have proved remarkably accurate in estimating the costs of tactical fighter aircraft programs. These equations may be found in *Methods of Estimating Fixed-Wing Airframe Costs,* Vol. 1 (Revised), PRC R-547A, Prepared for the Office of the Secretary of Defense under contract by the Planning

the one submitted on September 10, 1962, the Boeing Company stipulated that the thrust reversers were to be provided by the engine manufacturer, Pratt-Whitney, but *it* estimated the price which Pratt-Whitney would charge. This estimate was $40 million for the total cost (two reversers for each of the 1,700 planes) and $8,300 for each unit. This price for a yet undeveloped thrust reverser to be used on a combat plane for in-flight maneuvering — something which had never been done — was from 25 to 55 per cent lower than the price that the commercial airlines were paying to Boeing to furnish them with *its* already tested and proven thrust reverser that was used only during landings by jet transports.[44] Moreover, though the Boeing Company had experience with producing thrust reversers for commercial uses, so had three other companies — Pratt-Whitney, Rohr, and General Electric. Boeing's price for the TFX thrust reverser was 91 per cent lower than Pratt-Whitney's (theirs was $100,000 per unit), 76 per cent lower than Rohr's, and 76 per cent lower than General Electric's.[45]

McNamara hence added $100 million to Boeing's estimate of $40 million as the total cost of thrust reversers. (As a standard of comparison, after the contract was awarded, Pratt-Whitney estimated that it would cost $425 million to equip the General Dynamics-Grumman TFX with thrust reversers.)[46] He also estimated that Boeing's extensive use of titanium — a very expensive

---

Research Corporation (Los Angeles, 1961). ("Fixed wing" includes aircraft but excludes helicopters. It does include variable-sweep wing aircraft.)

Another of these steps was to involve Systems Analysis (SA) more in the actual making of development decisions than they appear to have been in the early stages of the TFX program. If DDR & E has asked whether it is technically and technologically *feasible* to build a new weapon system, then SA has asked, first, is it *necessary* to do so and, second, what operational features *should* the system have to meet the mission requirements it was designed for. McNamara thus involved people at the beginning of a new program who would ask the kind of questions he considered vital. (Such a thing was done in the C-5A military aircraft transport program.) It was through steps like these that McNamara tried to build into the development decision-making process methods and pressures that would produce the analyses and results that he wanted.

metal — would increase the cost of each plane by $50,000 and result in adding $85 million (for 1,700 planes) to the Boeing estimate.[47]

A third indication of Boeing's optimism was offered by Secretary Zuckert. He referred to something called man-hours per pound. This figure represents the ratio of the labor necessary to manufacture and assemble a given airframe to the weight of the airframe. The man-hours-per-pound ratio is used as a rough indicator for estimating costs in the airframe industry.* Boeing's estimate of its man-hours-per-pound ratio for the TFX was 20.† The historical average of the airframe industry was 26 for fighters. Boeing's figure was therefore about 23 per cent below the industry's average.[48] Boeing had apparently based its estimates on its experience with producing bombers. It had beaten the industry average there by about 30 per cent for man-hours per pound. However, its experience was based mainly on the B-47 and B-52, both of which had extremely long production runs that reduced unit costs, and both of which did not embody relatively large technological advances, as, for example, the B-58 bomber did. Moreover, as Zuckert said, Boeing's experience with producing bombers was neither comparable nor translatable to the production of fighters, especially those like the TFX, which embodied such large technological advances. The TFX fighter is a high-density (i.e., a great deal of electronic equipment is packed into it), super-

---

* The man-hours-per-pound ratio does not, however, express the labor cost necessary to manufacture a pound of airframe for this reason: the airframe manufacturing process includes the installation and assembly of both government-furnished and contractor-furnished equipment. Airframe weight, however, as defined, excludes the weight of the government-furnished equipment. Thus the man-hours include the time required to install and assemble equipment whose weight is not included in the airframe weight. This is the reason why the ratio does not measure the labor necessary to manufacture one pound of airframe. Nevertheless, as a rough cost indicator, the ratio remains valid.

† Boeing's estimate was actually 20.2. The Air Force estimate of the man-hours per pound for the TFX was 38. The General Dynamics-Grumman team's estimate of the TFX man-hours per pound was 21. It was therefore not significantly better than Boeing's.

sonic aircraft, whereas the B-47 and B-52 bombers were low-density, subsonic aircraft. Finally, not only was this bomber experience "untranslatable," but also Boeing had had no experience in producing modern fighters. The last fighter Boeing had made was the P-26, in 1939. The company had never built a supersonic fighter. Yet, its man-hours-per-pound estimate for the TFX was lower than that for any modern aircraft, even less than those for the P-38 and P-47 of World War II![49]

On the other hand, when he turned to the General Dynamics-Grumman proposal, though what he saw was not encouraging, it nevertheless indicated a better understanding of the costs involved. This team had taken a conservative approach in estimating the costs of the development program. It had planned for a relatively higher level of engineering and test effort. It had relied less on unknown processes and materials (like titanium). It had not complicated the already complex development effort by undertaking to incorporate features into the TFX that were not essential for meeting the services' performance specifications.[50] McNamara concluded that the team's greater cost realism reflected the extensive experience that both partners had had in producing fighter aircraft. The General Dynamics Corporation had developed, tested, and produced the F-102 and F-106, both supersonic fighters that were used extensively by the Air Force. The Grumman Aircraft Company had produced more than 25,000 aircraft since 1939, 23,500 of which had been carrier-based fighter aircraft. Half of the flying hours compiled by the Navy since World War II had been done in Grumman aircraft. It had produced the carrier-based, supersonic F11-F-1 fighter in 1954 and the F11-F-1F carrier-based, mach 2 fighter-bomber in 1956.[51] Together, the General Dynamics Corporation and Grumman Aircraft constituted a team that possessed extensive experience in developing both Air Force and Navy supersonic fighters. The Boeing Company had neither.

Based upon calculations of this type, McNamara became convinced that the Boeing approach for developing the TFX was inherently the more expensive one. Yet he found that the Boeing development bid was $145 million *less* than its competitor's.* In other words, he concluded that the Boeing approach would ultimately cost more, even though its bid on paper was less. The *exact* amount of the difference between the two bids was of no importance because of the unreliability of the bids. But there was a difference and Boeing's was the lower, proving to McNamara that Boeing was being highly optimistic and perhaps purposely underestimating its costs in order to buy into the program.

FPIF Contracts and the Bidders' Cost Estimates. If this was McNamara's judgment on the cost difference between the two proposals, what was the judgment of the military officers? Obviously, they could not deny that the Boeing proposal would involve development costs greater than the General Dynamics-Grumman one. The former offered a plane superior in performance, whose extras would entail added costs. Moreover, the officers had the judgment of the Evaluation Group before them that the General Dynamics-Grumman team had offered the more realistic bid. Finally, the results of their own weighted scores stared them in the face: General Dynamics-Grumman, 150.2; Boeing, 135.3. To deny that the General Dynamics-Grumman bid was the more realistic would thus have been to discredit both their own judgment and the value of System Source Selection.

The military officers wanted the Boeing plane. How could they then deal with this fact: it was likely to be the more expensive to develop? They resorted to two arguments. The first was characterized by General Le May's remark that "the operational advantages of the Boeing proposal outweighed the other factors involved" (p. 118). Thus the first argument was that the added performance was worth the extra cost. The officers urged its

---

* $711 million minus $576 million. The Air Force adjusted figures have been used here because even though McNamara felt they were too low, they at least gave a better idea of the respective cost of each proposal than anything else he had before him.

choice in spite of its expense. (After all, it was the greater expense that would produce the superior performance.) The second argument was to accept the fact that the Boeing design would be more expensive and that it would be much more so than Boeing had estimated, but to deny that the government would have to bear the increased costs. The officers pointed out that the FPIF contract would make the Boeing Company bear these increased costs. What difference did it make to the government, then, whether Boeing's bid was the more optimistic and whether it would prove to be the more expensive? In fact, why should the government not accept the optimistic, lower proposed bid? It would save money by doing so.

The first argument was valid in principle. That is, the increase in performance might be worth the increase in costs. To the military officers it obviously was. To McNamara and the civilian secretaries it obviously was not. This question was one of judgment, which turned on whether the increased operational capability on the one hand or the increased development risks on the other were emphasized. The second argument, however, was not valid. It was not true that the government would save money by accepting the more optimistic bid, for at least three reasons. First, Boeing's cost optimism *would* cost the government more money. Under the FPIF development contract for the TFX, the government would have to pay 90 per cent of the cost overruns up to 20 per cent over the target cost. If the development contract were signed with Boeing for $577 million, then the amount of allowable overrun that the government and Boeing would share could run as high as $116 million. Under the 90-10 per cent sharing formula, the government could pay as much as $104.4 million in additional costs over and above the original $577 million contract price.

Second, the FPIF contract did not make the contractor responsible for engineering changes (those which the Air Force had tried to take account of in its adjusted estimates of the contractors' bids). These changes were called "extra-scope" changes because they were not included in the initial development contract. Rather they were changes in the design upon which the contract was originally negotiated. Because the initial contract did not provide for these changes, the government had to bear all their costs in the form of add-ons to the contract price.[52] Extra-scope changes occurred in any complex development program, but their number and their side effects (such as causing other additional extra-scope changes or delaying the development schedule) usually increased with the complexity of the weapon system. Because the Boeing design was the more complex, it would probably require proportionately more extra-scope changes.[53] Moreover, because Boeing had not provided sufficient cost allowances for its technically more risky development approach, it might be forced to undertake many more such design changes than otherwise would have been necessary. For example, if it found that it was unable to produce a reliable thrust reverser in the necessary time, it might be forced to substitute spoilers. These in turn would require changes to the original design (built around the thrust reversers). Thus cost optimism could increase the number of extra-scope changes, increase their costs, and increase the likelihood of their occurring.

Third, the FPIF contract could not force Boeing to maintain its originally proposed level of quality during the development phase or prevent it from recouping any development losses during the follow-on production phase. If Boeing found that its development costs were much higher than it had anticipated, perhaps running into several hundreds of millions of dollars, it would be strongly motivated to introduce all possible cost-saving alternatives open to it. One of these might be reducing the plane's performance quality.[54] (Another could be delaying the date of operational delivery.) Or, if Boeing decided not to cut the plane's quality and hence sustained huge losses on the development of the TFX, it might try to recoup them by raising the price of the production contract.[55] Because both contracts were signed separately, because the production contract was not signed until the development contract had almost expired, because the estimates for the production contract, offered when the development contract was signed, were not legally binding, and because the government was virtually forced to award the production contract to the company that had received the development contract, the government might find itself paying for Boeing's cost optimism in spite of the stipulations of the FPIF development contract. Thus, since the development contract would be only about 12 per cent of the government's total outlay on the TFX, the incentive provisions of the FPIF development contract, burdening Boeing with the costs of its own optimism, might not be strong enough to dissuade it either from buying into the production contract, or from increasing its price for that contract once it had done so, or from cutting quality during development.

That the incentives would be stronger for the Boeing Company than for its competitor either to cut quality during development or to recoup development losses on the production contract can be readily seen by comparing their respective bids with the Air Force estimating standards. (That these standards might be lower than they should be only strengthens the following argument: it would make each bid even more optimistic.) In Tables 5.3 and 5.4 are illustrated two ways of comparing the bids to the standards — by amount and by percentage. According to the first, the contract ceiling price for the General Dynamics-Grumman team would be 120 per cent of the $711 million target price, or $853 million. Assume for the moment that the Air Force standards do in fact represent what the final development costs of the TFX will be. Then this team would have to bear 100 per cent of the remaining costs, or $65 million. For the Boeing Company the contract ceiling price would be 120 per cent of its target price of $577 million, or $692 million. It would have to bear 100 per cent of the remaining $181 million. Thus, because of its greatest cost optimism (its lower price), the Boeing Company would have to sustain a cost

TABLE 5.3. *R & D Cost Overruns for the TFX — Amounts*

	Air Force estimating standards	Air Force adjusted estimates (target cost)	Amount of allowable overrun (20% of column 2)	Ceiling price[a] (columns 2 + 3)	Contractor's burden[a] of overrun (columns 1 − 4
	(1)	(2)	(3)	(4)	(5)
General Dynamics- Grumman	918[b]	711	142	853	65
Boeing	873	577	115	692	181

[a] For illustrative purposes, the 90–10 per cent sharing formula has been ignored.

[b] Figures rounded off to nearest millions of dollars.

TABLE 5.4. *R & D Cost Overruns for the TFX — Percentages*

	Air Force estimating standards	Air Force adjusted estimates (target cost)	Amount of overrun (columns 1 − 2)	Percent- age of overrun (columns 3/2)	Percent- age of excess over allowable overrun (column 4 − 20%)
	(1)	(2)	(3)	(4)	(5)
General Dynamics- Grumman	918[a]	711	207	29.1	9.1
Boeing	873	577	296	51.3	31.3

[a] Figures rounded off to nearest millions of dollars.

overrun above and beyond its ceiling price that would be 2.8 times greater than that of the General Dynamics-Grumman team.

In Table 5.4 the same point is illustrated in percentages. Assume again that the Air Force standards represent the final development price. Then the amount of overrun for the General Dynamics-Grumman team would be $207 million. This figure would represent an overrun of 29.1 per cent over its target cost of $711 million. The amount of overrun for the Boeing Company would be $296 million, or 51.3 per cent over its target price of $577 million. When the 20 per cent of the overrun shared by the government and the contractor is subtracted, the General Dynamics-Grumman team would be 9.1 per cent over the allowable shared overrun (the ceiling price); the Boeing Company, 31.3 per cent over. By either calculation, then, the Boeing Company would be under monetary pressures much stronger than its competitor either to cut performance quality during development or to recoup its development losses during production.

As a result of these three factors, the Boeing Company's relatively greater optimism could in the long run cost the government more money than its competitor's optimism. McNamara was aware of all these factors, and in themselves they explain why he felt cost realism was so important to strive for.[56] But a fourth factor must have been in his mind, though he made no explicit reference to it, which made him concentrate on realism. That factor was this: his acceptance of such a highly optimistic bid probably would have reinforced the very thing that he was trying to prevent — cost optimism. By accepting competitive optimism in the first new weapons program he had initiated, especially one of such unprecedented size, he probably would have convinced the defense industry that he was indeed a "paper tiger," that all his words about the need for realistic development estimates were only that — words with no intent to back them up. According to his doctrine of cost effectiveness, competitive optimism led to inefficient decisions that misallocated scarce resources. Therefore, to have accepted the highly optimistic Boeing bid would have both encouraged future optimism and wasted present resources.

Thus McNamara made his decision on the cost proposals of the two competitors on these grounds:

(1) The contractors' estimates . . . [were] inadequate.
(2) The Air Force cost standards and resulting estimates . . . [were] inadequate.

(3) Design differences between the two planes probably would cause Boeing's cost to be higher.

(4) Throughout, Boeing's proposals pushed the state of the art further . . . greater incremental costs were inevitable because of the greater development risks and, even though impossible to quantify accurately, these costs would be substantial.

(5) . . . the greatest risk of all lay in the development of the swept wing. . . . It [was] not desirable to add to this fundamental risk the differential risk involved in Boeing's proposal with respect to relatively peripheral performance items.[57]

The military officers did not directly challenge any of these assumptions. Rather they argued that the improvement in performance justified the increase in costs, even if the government had to pay them. Again, McNamara looked at the development risks entailed in these performance extras — this time at their costs. Again the military officers looked at the promised performance extras — this time playing down their costs rather than playing up their benefits.

Commonality: Identical vs. Separate Planes

We can deal rather quickly with the third criterion by which McNamara judged the proposals of the two competitors. Commonality, it will be remembered, was the shorthand way of expressing the following idea: the degree to which each contractor's design provided for two structurally identical planes for both the Air Force and the Navy. In other words, commonality measured the degree to which each contractor deviated from one structural design in order to provide one version of the TFX to the Air Force and another version to the Navy. Commonality thus measured both the similarities and dissimilarities between the two versions of the contractor's basic design. McNamara, it will be recalled, had stated that he wanted "minimum divergence from a common design."

In Table 5.5 are summarized the findings of the Evaluation

149

The Evaluation

Group on the degree of commonality promised by the contractors' fourth-round designs. The design of the General Dynamics-Grumman team had 14,423 individual parts. Of these, 12,086, or 83.7 per cent, were identical parts: they could be used on either the Air Force or the Navy version. Identical parts were therefore interchangeable. By structural weight, the percentage of identical parts to total parts was even higher: 92 per cent. The design of the Boeing Company had 18,510 individual parts. Of these, 11,245 were identical parts, yielding a percentage of 60.7 by number and 34.0 by weight.

TABLE 5.5. *Summary of Commonality Estimates for the TFX*[a]

	Total number of parts	*Number of identical parts*	*Percentage of identical parts to total parts, by number*	*Percentage of identical parts to total parts, by structural weight*
General Dynamics-Grumman	14,423	12,086	83.7	92.0
Boeing	18,510	11,245	60.7	34.0

[a] These figures measure the parts and percentages on the Air Force versions. The figures are slightly different, but not significantly so, when the Navy versions are looked at. For example, the percentages of identical parts to total parts by number on the Navy versions are 80.2 per cent (12,086 to 15,059) for General Dynamics-Grumman and 60.4 per cent (11,245 to 18,605) for Boeing. (These percentages varied slightly from those given in the Air Force versions because of the larger number of parts in the Navy versions.)
Source: TFX Hearings, Vol. 1, p. 270; Vol. 8, p. 1986.

Obviously, the greater the number of identical parts a design had, the more nearly the two versions would resemble each other and therefore the less they would diverge from a common design. On the basis of this criterion, the Evaluation Group had concluded that Boeing

> . . . is in effect proposing two different airplanes from the structure point of view. . . . It is estimated that 60 percent of the

structural components of the wing, fuselage, and horizontal tail are different in the two versions. . . . This design approach has resulted in different Air Force and Navy airframes. . . .[58]

The two versions of the Boeing design (just like those of the General Dynamics-Grumman design) had never been *completely* identical, for there had been differences between them. The differences, however, had been in areas other than the wing, fuselage, and tail, in electronic equipment, for example. But because the wing, fuselage, and tail comprised the basic structure or airframe of the plane and because more than half the components of these parts were not identical, the Boeing design was in effect two structurally different designs, not two versions of one structural design. On the other hand, the Evaluation Group had concluded that the General Dynamics-Grumman design had

> . . . done a very good job of keeping the number of dissimilar or non-identical airframe structural components to a minimum. . . . Divergence has been limited to the areas required as a result of mission differences. . . . [for example] the radome and forward electronics compartment. . . . The airframe structure of the two versions is 92 percent identical.[59]

Thus, whereas Boeing proposed two planes, General Dynamics-Grumman proposed two versions of one plane.

This result had occurred because the two competitors had taken different approaches to solve the same problem during the fourth competition: how to meet the Navy's requirements for carrier compatibility. At the end of the second competition, the Navy had found both competitors' designs unsatisfactory because both planes had not met the wind-over-the-deck requirement of its carriers. With the Navy's stipulated wind-over-the-deck, neither company's version could have taken off from the carrier, either because of too much weight or too small a wing area or both. The two civilian service secretaries — Korth and Zuckert — at that time had recommended that McNamara allow some divergence in the airframe structures of the two versions; for only under this condition could a joint program have proceeded. Mc-Namara had agreed to do so and had informed the competitors of this decision for the third competition. But because the third competition had been so short, the contractors had not had enough time to develop their designs in the necessary detail. Consequently, a fourth competition had been ordered, with the same proviso: the contractors could allow their respective versions to diverge structurally in order to resolve the Navy's objections. It had been at this point that McNamara through Gilpatric had told the company presidents to keep the divergence from a common design to a minimum.

The Boeing Company had not done that because of the method it had chosen to meet the Navy's wind-over-the-deck requirement. It had chosen to reduce the weight of its Navy version by making that version's component parts lighter. To do this, it had proposed "to scale down the strength of the wings, fuselage, and tail by taking Air Force parts and machining as much of the structure away as was allowable."[60] By taking the parts of the Air Force version and "hogging out" (machining away) some of the metal in order to make the parts lighter, the Boeing Company had reduced the weight of its Navy version by 1,144 pounds.* But it had done so only at the cost of reducing the percentage of identical parts from 77 to 60.7.[61]

On the other hand, the General Dynamics-Grumman team had proposed to meet the Navy's wind-over-the-deck requirement, not by reducing the weight of the Navy version, but by increasing its wing area. It had retained the basic airframe structure of the Air Force version for its Navy version, but it had added three and one-half feet of wing span to the Navy version. It had done so by attaching bolt-on wingtip extensions to the wing structure of the Air Force version.[62] Comparing these two versions, the Evaluation Group had concluded that:

* Boeing had also made the Navy version lighter by using titanium extensively (pp. 123–124).

. . . the General Dynamics[-Grumman] approach of adding wing span . . . is more desirable than the Boeing approach of reducing the strength [by machining out parts]. . . . General Dynamics has a significant advantage in this area.[63]

McNamara analyzed the performance of the two competitors in the commonality area on the basis of these conclusions. He agreed with the Group's findings that the General Dynamics-Grumman design had the higher degree of identical airframe structure and that the Boeing design was in effect two different planes from the airframe structural standpoint.[64] Along with the Evaluation Group, he reasoned that the Boeing design would require more separate documentation for the two versions (that is, drawings; load, stress, and flutter analysis); more separate static, dynamic, and fatigue test programs for the two versions; and more extensive, separate developmental flight testing programs for the two versions. Two planes instead of one would increase the costs of the program at every point in development and would continue to do so throughout the production and support phases of the program (in the form of separate production lines, supply routes, supply storage points, etc.).[65] Finally, he reasoned that divergences in the early stages of a program usually grow larger as the program proceeds, while the incentive to retain the initial identity of parts increases during development. Because the General Dynamics-Grumman team offered the more nearly identical planes, McNamara concluded that it would be most likely to realize the cost savings inherent in a joint development approach.

On the other hand, the military officers favored the Boeing design precisely because it offered two structurally different airplanes instead of two versions of one basic airframe. Two planes would be better suited to each service's missions because their performance would not be compromised as much as that of two versions of one common plane. In short, Boeing's designs seemed more made to order for each service than those of its competitor. (For example, the Navy version of Boeing was 2,200 pounds

153

lighter than its competitor's Navy version.)⁶⁶ Because the military officers wanted the Boeing design, they resorted to the same argument that they had used for the cost criterion: the only possible justification for commonality was not in identical parts, but in the cost savings it would bring. Because the Boeing Company was offering the lower development and total program bid, any advantages that the General Dynamics-Grumman team might have over it in the commonality area would be negated by this fact.⁶⁷ The General Dynamics-Grumman team might in fact be offering two more nearly identical planes, but that made no difference: its cost estimate was still higher than Boeing's. Therefore, because Boeing offered a better plane and one better suited to each service and because it was still doing so with costs lower than those of its competitor, it should be chosen to develop the TFX.

McNamara thought these reasons as fallacious as he did those which the military had applied to the cost area. For he judged that the Boeing Company, since it could cut its quality during development or recoup its development losses during production, or both, had the more inherently expensive design but had offered the lower bid. That the company had offered the lower bid in the face of what appeared to be two separate development programs only strengthened McNamara's conclusion that the Boeing bid was much too optimistic. Once again each group saw different things when looking at the same two proposals. And once again both chose to emphasize differently the same things that they saw.

Having analyzed the extent to which both contractors met each of the three criteria (performance, cost, and commonality) upon which he had said he would judge their proposals, Secretary McNamara chose the General Dynamics-Grumman team to develop the TFX airplane. He explained the reasons for his choice in this way:

> The report itself [the Fourth Evaluation Report] did not express a preference for either proposal, and indicated there was little to choose between the proposals. Both proposals were certified by

General Le May and Admiral Anderson to meet military requirements. My examination of the facts, in consultation with my
advisors, convinced me that, as compared with the Boeing proposal, the General Dynamics proposal was substantially closer to
a single design, required only relatively minor modifications to
adapt it to the different requirements of the Navy and the Air
Force, and that it embodied a more realistic approach to the cost
problem. Accordingly, I decided to select General Dynamics as
the development contractor, since I concluded that it was best
qualified to design the most effective airplane that could be
produced at the least cost in the least time, to meet our military
requirements.[68]

McNamara chose in essence to *satisfy* the requirements that
the two services had agreed upon rather than to attempt to *exceed*
them with all the risks attendant on doing so. He thus chose to
"satisfice" the services' requirements rather than to meet their
"desirements."[69] Faced with a similar situation several months
later, McNamara stated clearly the general philosophy that lay
behind this choice:

> . . . this is what we do all the time. . . . *We don't buy the*
> *best there is in terms of technology in any one of our weapon*
> *systems.* We would be fools. No one does. The farmer did not
> buy the best truck. I didn't buy the best automobile. We would
> be foolish if we bought the best in technology in terms of the
> most advanced, in terms of speed and range and firepower, when
> we don't need it . . . the fact is that we have not bought the
> best in terms of modern technology because we don't need it.
> *We should buy only what we need.* . . .[70]

Two F-111A's, with their variable-sweep wings in the mach 2.5 configuration.

SIX · McNAMARA AND THE TFX: INNOVATIONS IN AN INSTITUTION

Types of Decisions

We began this book by asking two basic questions. First, why did Secretary of Defense Robert McNamara choose the General Dynamics Corporation to develop the TFX airplane when the chief of staff of the Air Force and the chief of Naval Operations both recommended that he select the Boeing Company to do the job? Second, why was he able to make and carry out such a decision when these two military chiefs had traditionally been the final authorities responsible for selecting sources to develop major weapon systems for their respective services?

We have answered the first question. In discussing the specific reasons for his choice, we saw that McNamara's institutional role and his analytical approach to making decisions led him to make such a choice. Furthermore, we saw that his analytical approach reinforced his institutional role. His institutional perspective required that he look at all the programs of the Defense Department in their relationships to each other. His cost-effectiveness technique made it possible for him to do so.[1] As secretary of

Defense, McNamara had ultimate responsibility for making certain that the country had integrated, balanced, and effective forces. He employed a technique of analysis (1) that required him to consider alternative ways of satisfying a military requirement, (2) that required him to calculate the cost of each alternative, (3) that required him to weigh the military effectiveness of each alternative, and (4) that required him to compare all alternatives in terms of their cost and effectiveness. By using such a technique, McNamara accomplished something that no secretary of Defense before him had done. He developed the ability to make informed decisions on which of the choices before him would contribute the most to integrating and balancing military instruments of force.

Intuition and hunches — the major methods of his predecessors — were still necessary for making decisions;* but these two could now be based upon a more complete, detailed knowledge both of what the military requirements were and of the options available to meet them. In systematically looking for and comparing options, McNamara acquired the information necessary to do his job effectively.

Secretary McNamara's goal did not differ from that of his military chiefs. He, as they, wanted to provide the country with the "best" possible defense. He, as they, believed that this was done by creating integrated and balanced forces. He, as they, thought that such forces required "adequate" and "suitable" weapon systems. However, what Secretary McNamara defined as "adequate" (the General Dynamics proposal), the service chiefs defined as satisfactory but less than desirable. What Secretary McNamara defined as "suitable" (the biservice approach), the service chiefs defined as possible but undesirable. The differences were thus not over the goals to be achieved but rather over the means by which to achieve them.

---

* Intuition and hunches were particularly necessary for McNamara's decisions on the TFX. See the note on pp. 138 and 139 (Chapter Five) and the note on p. 165 in this chapter.

In the TFX case, McNamara argued, first, that paying more for a weapon system *than was necessary in order to meet the military requirement* would mean that fewer resources would be available to spend on other weapon systems necessary to meet other military requirements. In so arguing, Secretary McNamara did not assert that the cheapest weapon system was always the "best" choice for meeting a particular requirement. The cheapest system might not yield the performance necessary to carry out a mission effectively. To choose the cheapest in such a case would mean in reality to choose the most expensive, both because the requirement would not have been met and because additional resources would have to be committed to meet the still unmet requirement. Rather, in picking the General Dynamics proposal, McNamara asserted one of his major management principles for running the Defense Department: that in a situation where each of two weapon systems meets the requirements, it is good *military* judgment to select the cheaper one.

Secretary McNamara argued, second, that making the TFX a biservice or common program, *when doing so would not prevent the two services from meeting their requirements,* would enable him to buy still more planes, if that proved necessary, than would have been possible had he chosen two completely different aircraft for the two services. In so arguing, Secretary McNamara did not assert that all new development programs should be carried out on a biservice or a triservice basis. In some situations such programs could prevent the services from meeting their requirements.* Again, such a choice, though it might appear to save money, could in the end be costlier. Rather, in making the TFX a biservice program, McNamara asserted a second of his major management principles for running the Defense Department: where one weapon

---

* It is precisely on this question, particularly on the effectiveness of the Navy's F-111B, that the TFX debate since 1963 has centered. If the Source Selection decision of November, 1962 has received more publicity, the biservice decision of September, 1961 has more consequences for service role and weapon system effectiveness.

system meets the requirements of several services, it is good *military* judgment to make the program a biservice one.

By his source selection and biservice decisions, McNamara in effect said to the two services: if you pay more than you have to for this weapon system, you will have fewer resources to purchase the other things that you need now or will need in the future. He thereby pressed them to consider, first, how much performance they really needed in a weapon system, not how much they ideally wanted, and, second, what effect choosing the more or the less expensive program would have on their present programs and future options. By these two basic decisions in the TFX program, Secretary McNamara required each service to consider what effect its development program would have not only on that of the other service but also on those of the entire Defense Department. Neither their experiences nor their institutional roles had predisposed the service chiefs to make such calculations. McNamara, in effect, asked each service chief to assume the perspectives of the secretary of Defense. That McNamara encountered so much opposition to the two basic TFX decisions was proof of how little accustomed the services were to considering such factors, and of how difficult their institutional perspectives made such a task for them.[2]

Control Over Decisions

Secretary McNamara, however, did more than ask the services to do things that they had never really tried. He also succeeded in making them do those things, where others before him had usually failed. This raises the second basic question of this book: how did McNamara make the services do what they had often claimed as their aim but had never worked for? How did he assert his authority over what had been considered military prerogative: the right to choose weapons and to select their producers?

First, he centralized the process of decision-making by deciding himself whenever it became evident to him that others would not make the kinds of decisions he wanted. Second, he altered certain elements in the decision-making process in order to make it produce in the future the types of decisions he wanted. By centralizing and altering the decision-making process, McNamara gained effective control over the key decisions that were being made in the Defense Department. He thus enlarged the effective power of the secretary of Defense both to make more decisions and to do so in areas hitherto untouched by persons in that office. He did so within the Defense Department generally and in the TFX case specifically.

Centralizing the Process. Centralizing decision-making power within the Office of the Secretary of Defense did not begin with McNamara. It had been a gradual development ever since the Department of Defense had been created in 1947.* What was new with McNamara was the efficiency and the effectiveness with which he accelerated this postwar trend. In part this acceleration was due to McNamara's own brilliance; in part, to the ability of the assistants he brought with him. But in larger part it was brought about by the curious reversal of positions that he produced within the Defense Department.

The revolutionary manner in which McNamara made his decisions (revolutionary, that is, for the Defense Department), transformed the "expert" career bureaucrat into the "novice" and the "inexperienced" political appointee into the "professional." By demanding that decisions be made through a cost-effectiveness analysis, McNamara freed himself from the secretary's usual dependence on the experience and knowledge of the military officer and the career civil servant. By demanding something that only he and his small personal staff possessed the experience and com-

* Technically, the Department of Defense was not created until 1949. What was called the National Military Establishment was created by the National Security Act of 1947. I am using the name "Department of Defense" here to encompass the three military services, the Joint Chiefs of Staff, the Office of the Secretary of Defense, and the Defense Department superagencies. For a clear discussion of the evolutionary development of the Defense Department since 1947, see John C. Reis, *The Management of Defense* (Baltimore: Johns Hopkins University Press, 1964).

petence to do, McNamara declared insufficient or invalid, or both, the customary criteria for making decisions and the traditional grounds for justifying them.

In the TFX case, McNamara refused to accept the judgment of the services either that a biservice program was not feasible or that the Boeing Company was preferable. Particularly in the latter case, McNamara asserted his independence from the bureaucracy. He refused to accept a decision sanctified by the repeated ratification of people who took very little time or trouble to make their decisions. Only one person other than Air Force Secretary Zuckert had even bothered to read the Fourth Evaluation Group Report. Most had not even glanced at it. Instead they had relied on an oral briefing that optimistically described the performance of the Boeing plane, but omitted the Report's critical analysis of the risks and difficulties involved in attempting to achieve such performance.* On the Fourth Round the members of the Source Selec-

---

* Zuckert stated that this habit of relying on an oral briefing rather than reading the Evaluation Group Report had become so standardized that he had to ask specifically for that report. It was not given to him as a matter of course in his review of the Source Selection Board's recommendation. Admiral Ashworth (a member of the Board), in an exchange with Senator McClellan in the 1963 *TFX Hearings* illustrated very well the practice of the military officers in these source selection decisions:

ADMIRAL ASHWORTH. I have never read the fourth evaluation report, sir. . . . It was not available to me in time to read it and it was not before the Source-Selection process.
CHAIRMAN MCCLELLAN. You mean you did not have that?
ADMIRAL ASHWORTH. I did not have access to it; no, sir.
CHAIRMAN MCCLELLAN. It was not provided.
ADMIRAL ASHWORTH. It was provided at the meeting of the Source Selection Board in the room in which we met.
CHAIRMAN MCCLELLAN. You mean that you had not an opportunity to read it?
ADMIRAL ASHWORTH. I had not had an opportunity to read it; no, sir.
CHAIRMAN MCCLELLAN. . . . Had it been provided before that day? . . . You did not have it before that time?
ADMIRAL ASHWORTH. No, sir.
CHAIRMAN MCCLELLAN. You had no opportunity to consider it?
ADMIRAL ASHWORTH. I have not personally had custody of a copy of that report and it was not available in the Bureau of Naval Weapons until January [of 1963].

tion Board did not receive this 400-odd page, highly technical report until the morning of the day they made their decisions.[3] Thus the biservice and source selection decisions were centrally imposed from the top down rather than "bubbling-up" from below. They were *McNamara's* decisions.

Altering the Process. There was, however, a danger to McNamara in making decisions in such a manner. In reversing the unanimous recommendation of his military officers, McNamara laid himself open to the charge of ignoring the judgment of experts who supposedly knew most about these matters. Such charges were made by Defense Department officials and by congressmen. In order to make certain that he would not be put in such a position

---

CHAIRMAN MCCLELLAN. You mean until after this investigation got underway?

ADMIRAL ASHWORTH. That is correct.

CHAIRMAN MCCLELLAN. *Why did you get it then?*

ADMIRAL ASHWORTH. *Because we wanted to see what was in it, because it apparently is the source for most of the facts . . . that are being used in the justification of the source selection. We wanted to read it.*

CHAIRMAN MCCLELLAN. You wanted to read it?

ADMIRAL ASHWORTH. We wanted to find out what was in it.

CHAIRMAN MCCLELLAN. *Had you had this before you at the time would you have changed your mind?*

ADMIRAL ASHWORTH. *No, sir; absolutely not.*

CHAIRMAN MCCLELLAN. *Even after reading it, after the fact?*

ADMIRAL ASHWORTH. *I have not read it, sir. . . .*

CHAIRMAN MCCLELLAN. *If you have not read it, how do you know you would not change your mind? . . . There may be something in there that is very vital here.*

ADMIRAL ASHWORTH. *No, sir, because I get my technical advice from my technical experts in the Bureau of Naval Weapons, and as far as I am concerned, my decisions are based upon that information. . . . My decision was [also] based upon the briefings that I received . . . the intent of the briefing by the Evaluation Group was a summary of that document.* (Vol. 3, pp. 650–52. Italics added.)

Thus, although the Evaluation Group spent hundreds of thousands of man-hours preparing their Report, the military officers did not bother to read it. What was in theory an exhaustive review of contractor proposals by these military officers became in reality a quick decision based upon a few minutes of an oral briefing that in the operational section constituted a statement of the reasons to support the Boeing design. No wonder, then, that Secretaries Zuckert and McNamara were suspicious of this process.

The Evaluation

FIGURE 6.1 *System Source Selection Procedure*

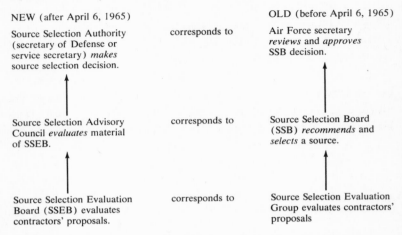

NEW (after April 6, 1965)

OLD (before April 6, 1965)

Source Selection Authority (secretary of Defense or service secretary) *makes* source selection decision.

corresponds to

Air Force secretary *reviews* and *approves* SSB decision.

Source Selection Advisory Council *evaluates* material of SSEB.

corresponds to

Source Selection Board (SSB) *recommends* and *selects* a source.

Source Selection Evaluation Board (SSEB) evaluates contractors' proposals.

corresponds to

Source Selection Evaluation Group evaluates contractors' proposals

again, McNamara resolved to strengthen his control over the process by which sources for the development of advanced weapon systems are selected. He did so in two ways. First, he made it impossible that he would ever again have to reverse the recommendation of his military officers by making it their function to *advise* him on the selection of sources rather than to *recommend* one to him. He would no longer have to overrule the military's recommendations because they could no longer make any. Second, he made clear through new regulations that the secretary of Defense was responsible for selecting the source, though he might choose to delegate the authority to one of the service secretaries. Through both changes McNamara canceled the ability of the Source Selection Board to make decisions for him.* He "rigged" the decision-making procedures in order to prevent them from blocking the out-

---

* These two changes apply to programs that will involve either $25 million or more for RDT & E or $100 million or more for production. Most major weapon system programs involve expenditures of such size in both categories. See Air Force Regulation No. 70–15, *Proposal Evaluation and Source Selection Procedures 20 September 1965;* and Department of Defense Directive No. 4105.62, *Proposal Evaluation and Source Selection 6 April 1965.*

comes he wanted. Figure 6.1 illustrates these two changes in the System Selection procedure by showing the correspondence between the old and new procedures.*

---

* McNamara faced a second danger by making decisions in such a manner: he put aside as almost totally useless for making the TFX source selection decision the information that the services were giving to him. But he did so *before* his own staff had the backlog of its own cost experience and statistical techniques that would have produced the type of information he would have considered useful. McNamara thus lay himself open to what he was accused of by Congress: making only "rough judgments" unsupported by detailed analysis in order to come to a decision. McNamara himself admitted to doing so. In fact, he was the one who used the phrase "rough judgment."

McNamara relied upon such judgments because he believed he had no other alternative. He reasoned that neither the services nor his staff as yet (in 1962) had the resources to produce what he would have considered valid estimates of aircraft development and production costs. (See Chapter Five, pp. 138–139, for an extended discussion of this point.) In this sense, therefore, McNamara did not have *all* the information he wanted to make the source selection decision. He did not have the resources to go through an extensive cost-effectiveness analysis. But he made the best of the cost estimates that were available to him. He did an *intuitive* cost-effectiveness analysis. Weighing the extra costs necessary to yield the extra promised increases in performance above the mission requirements against the desirability or military worth of such increases — this was a cost-effectiveness approach. It was a relatively crude analysis when compared to the ones he made on comparable programs in later years. The TFX, however, was the first major development program begun by McNamara and came early in his administration.

The TFX source selection decision at the same time was typical and atypical of his later style — typical because it contained the main elements of his decision-making approach; atypical because it was not performed with the same rigor and thoroughness with which he made most of his other decisions. In this sense the TFX program represents a watershed decision: it shows the Defense Department in transition. McNamara, as well as the military officers, learned from their experience with this program. Therefore, how critical one wishes to be of the fact that McNamara relied upon rough judgments to select General Dynamics-Grumman instead of Boeing to develop the TFX depends upon these factors: (1) to what extent one judges McNamara's actions in 1962 from hindsight; (2) to what extent one finds reasonable and credible his reasons for having to rely upon such rough judgments; and (3) how extensive one thinks cost-effectiveness analyses can and should be when applied to development programs.

Thus what is important for this study is not the *extent* of McNamara's analysis on this decision, but rather *why* he felt he was forced to rely on rough judgments, the *manner* in which he made and used these judgments, and the *changes* he made in order to avoid having to rely on such rough judgments in the future. (See Chapter Five, p. 139, for two of these changes.)

Conceptions of the Office

In the TFX program, then, Secretary of Defense McNamara inno-
vated both in the types of decisions that he did make and in the
manner in which he made and carried them out. Both types of
innovations stemmed from a conception that McNamara had of his
office — a conception unlike that of any of his predecessors, except
perhaps for that of James Forrestal. In making such novel decisions and in enforcing them, McNamara in effect not only asserted
that a secretary of Defense can make and overrule decisions on
military as well as financial and administrative grounds. He also
asserted that because any analytic technique can yield only so
much information, it is necessary for a decision maker to make
judgments and that his perspective as secretary of Defense made
his judgments the most valuable and valid for the requirements of
his job.[4] In order to innovate McNamara had to take the initiative.
In his own words:

> I think that the role of public manager is very similar to the
> role of a private manager; in each case he has the option of fol-
> lowing one of two major alternative courses of action. He can
> either act as a judge or a leader. In the former case, he sits and
> waits until subordinates bring to him problems for solution, or
> alternatives for choice. In the latter case he immerses himself in
> the operations of the business or governmental activity, examines
> the problems, the objectives, the alternative courses of action,
> chooses among them, and leads the organization to their ac-
> complishment. In the one case, it's a passive role; in the other
> case, an active role. . . . *I have always believed in and en-
> deavored to follow the active leadership role as opposed to the
> passive judicial role.*[5]
>
> *I'm here to originate and stimulate new ideas and programs,
> not just to referee arguments.*[6]

In the TFX controversy that is exactly what he did.

BIBLIOGRAPHIC NOTES
(Identified in text by superior figures)

INTRODUCTION

1. U.S. Senate, Permanent Subcommittee on Investigation of the Committee on Government Operations, *The TFX Contract Investigation: Hearings,* 88th Cong., 1st Sess., 1963, Vol. 2, p. 443. (Hereafter referred to as the *TFX Hearings.*)

CHAPTER ONE

1. Testimony of General Sweeney, commander of the Tactical Air Command, in *TFX Hearings,* Vol. 3, pp. 738, 740.
2. R. A. Smith, "The 7-Billion Dollar Contract That Changed the Rules," *Fortune,* LXVII (March, 1963), 97–98.
3. *Ibid.,* p. 98.
4. Testimony of John Stack, *TFX Hearings,* Vol. 1, p. 15.
5. *Ibid.*
6. "Two Wings in One — Variable Sweep for Series Production," *Interavia,* XVII (May, 1962), 617.
7. "Assembling of TFX Subcontractors Begins," *Aviation Week and Space Technology,* LXXVII (December 3, 1962), 27.
8. *Ibid.* For a more detailed technical analysis of the aerodynamic factors involved in the variable-sweep wing, see "TFX: Mission and Design," *Space Aeronautics,* XXXIX (June, 1963), 72–83.
9. Smith, p. 99.
10. Testimony of Colonel Gregory, director of Requirements, Headquar-

ters, Tactical Air Command, Langley Air Force Base, Virginia, *TFX Hearings,* Vol. 3, p. 718.

11. Testimony of John Stack, *ibid.,* Vol. 1, pp. 14, 22.

12. Prepared statement of William M. Allen, president of the Boeing Company, *ibid.,* Vol. 4, p. 916.

13. Testimony of John Stack, *ibid.,* Vol. 1, p. 22.

14. "TFX: The Story Behind America's Largest Aircraft Program," *Interavia,* XVIII (November, 1963), 1694.

15. Testimony of Colonel Gregory, *TFX Hearings,* Vol. 3, p. 718.

CHAPTER TWO

1. See W. W. Kaufmann, *The McNamara Strategy* (New York: Harper and Row, 1964), Chaps. 2 and 5.

2. Charles J. Hitch, "Economics and Military Operations Research," *Review of Economics and Statistics,* XL (August, 1958), pp. 200–201.

3. *Ibid.,* p. 201.

4. R. A. Smith, "The 7-Billion Dollar Contract That Changed the Rules," *Fortune,* LXVII (March, 1963), 99–100.

5. Written statement by Secretary of Defense Robert S. McNamara, *TFX Hearings,* Vol. 2, p. 376. See also Hal Bamford, "What Managers Can Learn from the TFX," *Armed Forces Management,* IX (January, 1963), 16.

6. Prepared statement of Secretary of the Navy Fred Korth, *TFX Hearings,* Vol. 6, p. 1385.

7. Memorandum for the Director of Defense Research and Engineering from James H. Wakelin, Jr., on Aircraft for Close Air Support, Interdiction, Air Superiority and Reconnaissance, March 9, 1961, in *ibid.,* Vol. 6, p. 1462.

8. *Ibid.,* p. 1463.

9. Prepared statement of Secretary of the Navy Korth, *ibid.,* Vol. 6, p. 1385.

10. *Ibid.,* p. 1386.

11. See Larry Booda, "Defense Delays Final Decision on TFX," *Aviation Week and Space Technology,* LXXVI (February 5, 1962), 28; and W. T. Gunston, "TFX: A Next Generation Military Aeroplane," *Flight International,* LXXXI (February 8, 1962), 208.

12. Prepared statement of Secretary of the Navy Korth, *TFX Hearings,* Vol. 6, p. 1387.

13. Prepared statement of Secretary of the Air Force Eugene Zuckert, *ibid.,* Vol. 8, p. 1899.

14. Memorandum for the Record on the TFX Program by A. W. Blackburn, March 1, 1963, in *ibid.,* Vol. 5, p. 1203.

15. Prepared statement of Secretary of the Navy Korth, *ibid.,* Vol. 6, p. 1382.

16. Smith, p. 100.

17. Prepared statement of Secretary of the Navy Korth, *TFX Hearings,* Vol. 6, pp. 1377–78.

18. *Ibid.*

19. Smith, p. 100.

20. Booda, "Defense Delays Decision on TFX," p. 28.

21. Larry Booda, "Rift May Affect TFX Role," *Aviation Week and Space Technology,* LXXIX (September 9, 1963), 26.

22. Smith, p. 100.

23. Memorandum for the Secretary of Defense on Project 34 from Secretary of the Navy John B. Connally, May 31, 1961, in *TFX Hearings,* Vol. 6, pp. 1387–88.

24. Testimony of Dr. James H. Wakelin, *ibid.,* Vol. 6, p. 1476.

25. Prepared statement of Secretary of the Navy Korth, *ibid.,* Vol. 6, p. 1391; and Memorandum on TFX for the Secretary of Defense from Acting Secretary of the Navy Paul B. Fay, Jr., August 22, 1961, in Vol. 6, p. 1464.

26. Larry Booda, "USAF and Navy Unable to Agree on Joint Tactical Fighter Project," *Aviation Week and Space Technology,* LXXV (August 21, 1961), 27.

27. Prepared statement by Secretary of the Air Force Eugene Zuckert, *TFX Hearings,* Vol. 8, p. 1899.

28. Memorandum on TFX for the Secretary of Defense from Acting Secretary of the Navy Paul B. Fay, Jr., August 22, 1961, in *ibid.,* Vol. 6, p. 1465.

29. *Ibid.*

30. Prepared statement of A. W. Blackburn, *ibid.,* Vol. 5, pp. 1188–89.

31. Memorandum on TFX for the Secretary of the Air Force and the Secretary of the Navy, September 1, 1961, *ibid.,* Vol. 6, p. 1514.

32. *Ibid.*

CHAPTER THREE

1. Written statement by Secretary of Defense McNamara, *TFX Hearings,* Vol. 2, pp. 376–77.

2. The following paragraphs are based on these sources: (1) the *TFX Hearings,* Vol. 1, pp. 43–54, Vol. 2, pp. 453–54, and Vol. 3, pp. 759–60; (2) Norman Waks, "Selective Competition in New Air Weapon Procurement" (unpublished Ph.D. dissertation, Harvard Graduate School of Business Administration, 1961), Chap. 4, pp. 18–41; (3) Department of the Air Force, *The System Source Selection Process: A Descriptive Booklet* (undated), to be found as Exhibit No. 44 of the 1963 *TFX Hearings* in the Files of the Permanent Investigating Subcommittee of the Committee on Government Operations, U.S. Senate; (4) Department of the Air Force, Air Force Regulation No. 70-15, *System Source Selection Procedures 24 April 1962;* (5) Department of the Air Force, Air Force Regulation No. 80-3, System Source Selection Board, Wright-Patterson Air Force Base, Ohio, *Instructions to the Chairman of the Evaluation Group for System 324 A* (the TFX), to be found as Exhibit No. 80 of the 1963 *TFX Hearings* in the Files of the Permanent Investigating Subcommittee of the Committee on Government Operations, U.S. Senate; (6) Department of the Air Force, Air Force Manual No. 70-10, *System Source Selection Board Procedures 18 January 1963;* and (7) interviews with government and industry personnel familiar with this procedure.

3. For a discussion of how the System Source Selection procedure

compares with other methods of carrying on competitions to award weapons contracts, see Merton J. Peck and Frederic Scherer, *The Weapons Acquisition Process: An Economic Analysis* (Boston: Harvard Business School, 1962).

4. Larry Booda, "Defense Delays Decision of TFX," *Aviation Week and Space Technology*, LXXVI (February 5, 1962), 29.

5. Testimony of Colonel Gayle, *TFX Hearings*, Vol. 1, p. 54.

6. Larry Booda, "Final Decision of TFX Due Soon," *Aviation Week and Space Technology*, LXXVI (February 19, 1962), 31.

·7. R. A. Smith, "The 7-Billion Dollar Contract That Changed the Rules," *Fortune*, LXVII (March, 1963), 182.

8. *Ibid.*

9. Larry Booda, "Boeing Will Change Engine in TFX Bid," *Aviation Week and Space Technology*, LXXVI (February 12, 1962), 28.

10. Booda, "Final Decision on TFX Due Soon," p. 31.

11. Testimony of Admiral Frederick L. Ashworth, assistant chief of the Bureau of Naval Weapons, *TFX Hearings*, Vol. 2, p. 490.

12. Testimony of Colonel Gayle, *ibid.*, Vol. 1, pp. 55–56.

13. Testimony of Brigadier General Almond T. Culbertson, vice-commander of the Air Proving Ground Center and the Air Force Systems Command, *ibid.*, Vol. 2, pp. 465–66.

14. Written statement by Secretary of Defense McNamara, *ibid.*, Vol. 2, p. 378.

15. *Ibid.*

16. Testimony of Robert Emmett Dunne, assistant counsel for the McClellan Subcommittee, *ibid.*, Vol. 1, p. 59.

17. *Ibid.*

18. Prepared statement of Secretary of the Navy Korth, *ibid.*, Vol. 6, p. 1395.

19. Testimony of Admiral Ashworth, *ibid.*, Vol. 2, pp. 488–89.

20. Testimony of George Spangenberg, director of the Evaluation Division, Bureau of Naval Weapons, *ibid.*, Vol. 2, pp. 325–26.

21. Memorandum from the Chief of the Bureau of Naval Weapons to Wright-Patterson Air Force Base (Navy Evaluation of Second Proposals), May 1, 1962, in *ibid.*, Vol. 1, p. 58.

22. Testimony of Admiral Ashworth, *ibid.*, Vol. 3, p. 647.

23. Testimony of Robert Emmett Dunne, *ibid.*, Vol. 1, pp. 59–60; and testimony of Admiral Ashworth, *ibid.*, Vol. 2. p. 494.

24. Written statement by Secretary McNamara, in *ibid.*, Vol. 2, p. 379.

25. Memorandum for the Record on the TFX by A. W. Blackburn, March 1, 1963, in *ibid.*, Vol. 5, p. 1204.

26. Testimony of Admiral Ashworth, *ibid.*, Vol. 2, p. 513; and Memorandum from Secretary of the Air Force and Secretary of the Navy to the Secretary of Defense on the TFX Program, June 1, 1962, *ibid.*, Vol. 2, p. 513.

27. Written statement by Secretary of Defense McNamara, in *ibid.*, Vol. 2, p. 379; and prepared statement by Secretary of the Navy Korth, in *ibid.*, Vol. 6, p. 1398.

28. Prepared statement of Admiral Ashworth, *ibid.*, Vol. 2, pp. 498–99.

29. Memorandum for the Record on the TFX by A. W. Blackburn, in *ibid.*, Vol. 5, pp. 1204–1205; and testimony of Admiral Ashworth, *ibid.*, Vol. 2, pp. 511–12.

30. Memorandum for the Record on the TFX by A. W. Blackburn, in *ibid.*, Vol. 5, p. 1204.

31. Written statement by Secretary McNamara, *ibid.*, Vol. 2, pp. 379–80.

32. Memorandum for the Record on the TFX by A. W. Blackburn, in *ibid.*, Vol. 5, p. 1205.

33. Prepared statement of Secretary of the Navy Korth, *ibid.*, Vol. 6, p. 1399.

34. Written statement by Secretary McNamara, *ibid.*, Vol. 2, p. 380.

35. Memorandum to the Chairman of the Source Selection Board from Secretary of the Air Force Zuckert on the TFX Program, June 29, 1962, in *ibid.*, Vol. 1, p. 65.

36. Testimony of Colonel Gayle, *ibid.*, p. 66.

37. Letter from Deputy Secretary of Defense Gilpatric to the Presidents of the Boeing Company, Grumman Aircraft, and General Dynamics Corporation, July 13, 1962, in *ibid.*, Vol. 5, p. 1195.

38. R. A. Smith, "The 7-Billion Dollar Contract That Changed the Rules," *Fortune*, LXVII (April, 1963), p. 192.

39. *Ibid.*; and testimony of Robert Emmett Dunne, *TFX Hearings*, Vol. 1, pp. 73–75.

CHAPTER FOUR

1. Merton J. Peck and Frederic M. Scherer, *The Weapons Acquisition Process: An Economic Analysis* (Boston: Harvard Business School, 1962), p. 24.

2. Department of Defense, *Incentive Contracting Guide Prepared by the Office of Assistant Secretary of Defense for Installations and Logistics* (Washington, D.C.: U.S. Government Printing Office, 1963), p. 1.

3. Peck and Scherer, pp. 315–16.

4. Frederic M. Scherer, *The Weapons Acquisition Process: Economic Incentives* (Boston: Harvard Business School, 1964), pp. 132–33.

5. Carl Kaysen, "Improving the Efficiency of Military Research and Development," *Public Policy*, Vol. XII (Cambridge: Harvard Graduate School of Public Administration, 1963), p. 244.

6. Department of Defense, *Incentive Contracting Guide*, pp. 1–2.

7. Department of Defense, *Procurement Presentation to the Procurement Subcommittee of the Committee on Armed Services, U.S. Senate* (Washington, D.C.: Government Printing Office, 1960), p. 24.

8. Scherer, pp. 132–33.

9. *Ibid.*, pp. 134–35.

10. Testimony of Colonel Gayle, *TFX Hearings*, Vol. 1, p. 220.

11. Department of Defense, *Incentive Contracting Guide*, pp. 5, 12.

12. *Ibid.*, p. 5.

13. *Ibid.*, p. 6.

14. Richard Nelson, "Uncertainty, Learning, and the Economics of Par-

alleled Research and Development Efforts," *Review of Economics and Statistics,* XLIII (November, 1961), 352–53.

15. *Ibid.*

16. These points are developed in much greater detail in Peck and Scherer, pp. 325–26, and Norman Waks, "Selective Competition in New Air Weapon Procurement" (unpublished Ph.D. dissertation, Harvard Graduate School of Business Administration, 1961), Chap. 3, pp. 8–16.

17. Waks, Chap. 3, p. 11.

18. Peck and Scherer, pp. 412–13.

19. *Ibid.,* p. 416.

20. Written statement by Secretary of Defense McNamara, *TFX Hearings,* Vol. 2, pp. 375–76.

21. For an interesting discussion of the factors producing cost optimism and the success that incentive contracting can hope to have in combating them, see Scherer, pp. 153–90. Scherer's basic thesis is that the competitive pressures to meet time schedules and performance goals are stronger than the contractual incentives to estimate costs realistically before actual development begins. Hence he says that there will always be an element of optimism in a contractor's cost estimates that is produced by competition with other companies bidding for the contract.

22. Memorandum for Deputy Secretary of Defense from the Deputy Director of Defense Research and Engineering on Bidding and Source Evaluation Procedures, August 18, 1962, in *TFX Hearings,* Vol. 5, pp. 1295–96.

23. *Ibid.*

24. *Ibid.*

25. *Ibid.,* Vol. 3, p. 698.

26. The following discussion is based entirely on the *TFX Hearings.* See Vol. 1, pp. 52–53, 233, 238, 241; and Vol. 2, pp. 359, 365–69, 456–59, 461.

CHAPTER FIVE

1. Testimony of Colonel Gayle, *TFX Hearings,* Vol. 1, pp. 62, 63, 252.

2. Testimony of George Spangenburg, director of the Evaluation Division, Bureau of Naval Weapons, *ibid.,* Vol. 2, p. 366.

3. Testimony of General Ruegg, commander of the Aeronautical Systems Division, Air Force Systems Command, *ibid.,* Vol. 2, pp. 458–59.

4. *Ibid.,* Vol. 3, p. 619.

5. Summary of the Fourth Evaluation Report on the TFX Program, *ibid.,* Vol. 1, p. 147.

6. Conclusions: Summary of the Fourth Evaluation Report on the TFX Program, *ibid.,* Vol. 1, p. 146. (Italics added.)

7. Fourth Evaluation Report on the TFX Program: Navy Report on Carrier Compatibility, *ibid.,* Vol. 3, p. 734. (Italics added.)

8. Letter from General W. C. Sweeney, commander TAC to Headquarters, USAF, Washington, D.C., November 6, 1962, in *ibid.,* Vol. 3, p. 743.

9. *Ibid.,* p. 697.

10. Testimony of John Stack, *ibid.,* Vol. 1, p. 26.

11. Testimony of Colonel Gayle, *ibid.,* p. 186.

12. Testimony of John Stack, *ibid.*, pp. 31–33.
13. *Ibid.*
14. *Ibid.*, p. 34.
15. *Ibid.*, pp. 31–33.
16. Testimony of Admiral Ashworth, *ibid.*, Vol. 3, p. 650.
17. Testimony of John Stack, *ibid.*, Vol. 1, p. 29.
18. Written statement by Secretary McNamara, *ibid.*, Vol. 2, pp. 375–76.
19. *Ibid.*, p. 387.
20. *Ibid.*, Vol. 9, p. 2351.
21. General Carl "Tooey" Spatz, quoted in Robert Hotz, "Editorial: TFX," *Aviation Week and Space Technology*, LXXVIII (May 13, 1963), 21.
22. Prepared statement, *TFX Hearings*, Vol. 8, p. 1980.
23. Merton J. Peck and Frederic M. Scherer, *The Weapons Acquisition Process: An Economic Analysis* (Boston: Harvard Business School, 1962), p. 468; and testimony of Secretary of the Air Force Zuckert, *ibid.*, Vol. 9, p. 2355.
24. Written statement by Secretary McNamara, *TFX Hearings*, Vol. 2, p. 383.
25. Testimony of Dr. Charyk, under secretary of the Air Force, *ibid.*, Vol. 9, p. 2385.
26. Prepared statement of Secretary of the Air Force Zuckert, *ibid.*, Vol. 8, p. 1984.
27. Written statement by Secretary McNamara, *ibid.*, Vol. 2, pp. 383–84; prepared statement of Secretary of the Air Force Zuckert, *ibid.*, Vol. 8, p. 1980; and Colonel Gayle, Simulated Fourth Evaluation Briefing to the McClellan Subcommittee, *ibid.*, Vol. 8, p. 1936.
28. Fourth Evaluation Report on the TFX Program, *ibid.*, Vol. 8, p. 1981.
29. Testimony of Secretary of the Air Force Zuckert, *ibid.*, Vol. 9, p. 2447; and testimony of Dr. Charyk, *ibid.*, Vol. 9, p. 2340.
30. Interview with Eugene M. Zuckert, February 1, 1967.
31. Written statement by Secretary McNamara, *TFX Hearings*, Vol. 2, p. 384; and Fourth Evaluation Report on the TFX Program, *ibid.*, Vol. 8, pp. 1981–83.
32. Prepared statement of Secretary of the Air Force Zuckert, *ibid.*, Vol. 8, p. 1983.
33. Norman Waks, "Selective Competition in New Air Weapon Procurement" (unpublished Ph.D. dissertation, Harvard Graduate School of Business Administration, 1961), Chap. 7, pp. 20–21.
34. Conclusions: Summary of the Fourth Evaluation Report on the TFX Program, *TFX Hearings*, Vol. 1, p. 146.
35. *Ibid.*, Vol. 4, p. 1042.
36. Testimony of Air Force Secretary Zuckert, *ibid.*, Vol. 8, p. 2152.
37. Memorandum of GAO Interview with Secretary McNamara, April 16, 1963, *TFX Hearings*, Vol. 3, p. 902.
38. Letter from Joseph Campbell, comptroller general of the United States to Senator John L. McClellan, April 26, 1963, *ibid.*, Vol. 3, pp. 881–82; and letter from Secretary McNamara to John L. McClellan, April 5, 1963, *ibid.*, Vol. 3, p. 860.

39. Testimony of Hassell B. Bell, associate director of Defense Accounting and Auditing Division, General Accounting Office, *ibid.*, Vol. 3, p. 900.

40. Memorandum of GAO Interview with Secretary McNamara, April 16, 1963, *ibid.*, Vol. 3, p. 901.

41. *Ibid.*

42. *Ibid.*, p. 902.

43. *Ibid.*, p. 903.

44. Testimony of Secretary of the Air Force Zuckert, *ibid.*, Vol. 9, p. 2384.

45. *Ibid.*

46. "TFX Thrust Reverser — Cost, Weight Cited," *Aviation Week and Space Technology*, LXXVII (April 15, 1963), 30.

47. Memorandum of GAO Interview with Secretary McNamara, April 16, 1963, *TFX Hearings*, Vol. 3, p. 902.

48. See Memorandum for Secretary Zuckert on Price Analysis for the TFX by James E. Williams, Jr., assistant to the deputy assistant secretary, Air Force Systems and Production, November 7, 1962, *TFX Hearings*, Vol. 8, pp. 2190–92; and testimony of Mr. Brown, chief of the Pricing Branch of the Procurement and Production Staff, ASD, March 14, 1963, in "TFX Contract and Procurement Staff Interview," p. 33, to be found as Exhibit No. 56 of the 1963 *TFX Hearings* in the files of the Permanent Investigating Subcommittee of the Committee on Government Operations, U.S. Senate.

49. Testimony of Secretary of the Air Force Zuckert, *TFX Hearings*, Vol. 9, p. 2357 and Vol. 8, p. 2218.

50. Written statement by Secretary McNamara, *ibid.*, Vol. 2, p. 374.

51. Prepared statement of Roger M. Lewis, president and chief executive of the General Dynamics Corporation, *ibid.*, Vol. 4, pp. 1057–58.

52. Written statement by Secretary McNamara, *ibid.*, Vol. 2, pp. 385–86; and testimony of Secretary of the Air Force Zuckert, *ibid.*, Vol. 8, p. 1992.

53. Written statement by Secretary McNamara, *ibid.*, Vol. 2, pp. 385–86.

54. *Ibid.*

55. *Ibid.*, and testimony of Secretary of the Air Force Zuckert, *ibid.*, Vol. 8, p. 2156.

56. See his testimony before the McClellan Subcommittee, *ibid.*, Vol. 2, pp. 385–86.

57. Memorandum of GAO Interview with Secretary McNamara, April 16, 1963, *ibid.*, Vol. 3, p. 903.

58. Fourth Evaluation Report of TFX Program Officer, *ibid.*, Vol. 3, pp. 691–92.

59. *Ibid.*, p. 692.

60. Testimony of General Ruegg, *ibid.*, Vol. 3, pp. 614–15.

61. *Ibid.*, Vol. 4, p. 970; prepared statement by A. W. Blackburn, *ibid.*, Vol. 5, p. 1215; and testimony of Benjamin Gilleas, professional staff member of the Senate Preparedness Subcommittee of the Committee on Armed Services, *ibid.*, Vol. 1, p. 274.

62. Fourth Evaluation Report on the TFX Program, *ibid.*, Vol. 3, p. 692.

63. *Ibid.*, Vol. 8, p. 1986.

64. Written statement by Secretary McNamara, *ibid.*, Vol. 2, pp. 381–82.

65. *Ibid.*, p. 382; and Fourth Evaluation Report on the TFX Program, *ibid.*, Vol. 8, pp. 1986–87.

66. Testimony of Colonel Gayle, *ibid.*, Vol. 1, pp. 139–41.

67. Testimony of Admiral Ashworth, *ibid.*, Vol. 3, p. 658.

68. Written statement by Secretary McNamara, *ibid.*, Vol. 2, p. 375.

69. I owe this expression to Dr. Harold Brown. See his testimony as Secretary of the Air Force before the Department of Defense Subcommittee of the Committee on Appropriations, House of Representatives, *Hearings on the Department of Defense Appropriations for Fiscal Year 1964*, 88th Cong., 1st Sess., 1963, Part 6, p. 75.

70. Testimony before the Joint Atomic Energy Committee, *Hearings on Nuclear Propulsion for Naval Surface Vessels*, 88th Cong., 1st Sess., 1963, p. 171. (Italics added.)

CHAPTER SIX

1. This was not the only device that McNamara used to gain an overview of Defense Department programs. It is the crucial one for explaining his actions in the TFX controversy. For a good discussion of some of the other techniques he used, see Charles J. Hitch, *Decision-Making for Defense* (Berkeley: University of California Press, 1966), Chap. 2.

2. See Maxwell D. Taylor, *The Uncertain Trumpet* (New York: Harper and Bros., 1959), Chaps. 5, 6, and 7, and Hitch, Chap. 2, for two good discussions on how the military services had failed in the 1950's to achieve balanced forces through the mechanism of the Joint Strategic Objectives Plan (JSOP).

3. Testimony of John Rubel, *TFX Hearings*, Vol. 5, pp. 1319–20; and interview with Eugene M. Zuckert, February 1, 1967.

4. Richard Neustadt makes the same point about the presidency. See his *Presidential Power: The Politics of Leadership* (New York: John Wiley and Sons, 1960), Chap. 3.

5. Extract from the transcript of an interview with Secretary of Defense Robert S. McNamara on the National Broadcasting Company's program *Today*, February 17, 1961, quoted in Hitch, p. 27. (Italics added.)

6. Quoted in Eugene M. Zuckert, "The Service Secretary: Has He a Useful Role?" *Foreign Affairs*, XLIV (April, 1966), 464. (Italics added.)

APPENDIX

CHRONOLOGY OF KEY EVENTS IN THE TFX STORY

The First Phase: Origins

March, 1960	Stack of NASA finds variable-sweep wing feasible.
April, 1960	Air Research and Development Command, Tactical Air Command, and NASA agree at joint conference on program for TFX.
July 14, 1960	SOR 183 is drawn up for Air Force TFX with accompanying work statement.
October, 1960	Director of R & D orders holdup on source selection pending review by secretary of Defense.

The Second Phase: Commonality

February, 1961	McNamara says TFX should be made to fulfill requirements of Air Force, Navy, and Army.
June 7, 1961	McNamara concludes TFX should fulfill requirements of only Air Force and Navy.
August 22, 1961	Air Force and Navy report to McNamara

	they are unable to reach agreement over joint requirements for TFX.
September 1, 1961	McNamara unilaterally sets requirements for Air Force and Navy for TFX.
October 1, 1961	Air Force issues request for proposal and work statement to airframe industry.
December 1, 1961	Airframe companies submit their proposals to Source Selection Board.

The Third Phase: The Runoff

January 19, 1962	Source Selection Board votes unanimously to recommend Boeing as winner of TFX contract.
January 24, 1962	Air Force Council rejects Source Selection Board's decision and recommends eight-week extended competition between Boeing and General Dynamics-Grumman.
April 1, 1962	Boeing and General Dynamics-Grumman submit second proposals to Source Selection Board.
May, 1962	Source Selection Board (May 14) and Air Force Council (May 24) recommend award of contract to Boeing, but Navy refuses to go along.
Late May, 1962	Korth and Zuckert reject decision and order a third three-week competition between Boeing and General Dynamics-Grumman.
June 14, 1962	Boeing and General Dynamics-Grumman submit third proposals to Source Selection Board.
June 20–21, 1962	Source Selection Board and Air Force Council again recommend award of TFX contract to Boeing, but Navy refuses to go along.
July 1, 1962	McNamara orders final runoff between Boeing and General Dynamics-Grumman on basis of open "pay-off points."
September 11, 1962	Boeing and General Dynamics-Grumman submit their fourth and last proposals to Source Selection Board.

November, 1962	Source Selection Board (November 2) and Air Force Council (November 8) recommend award of TFX contract to Boeing.
November 13, 1962	Zuckert, Gilpatric, and McNamara decide tentatively to award contract to General Dynamics-Grumman.
November 24, 1962	Pentagon publicly announces award of TFX development contract to General Dynamics-Grumman team.

BIBLIOGRAPHY

I have relied primarily on these four sources in obtaining the details and the flavor of the TFX controversy: (1) the *Hearings on the TFX Contract Investigation* (10 volumes) held before the Permanent Subcommittee on Investigations of the Senate Committee on Government Operations, 88th Cong., 1st Sess., February–November, 1963 (Washington, D.C.: Government Printing Office, 1963–1964), as well as the files of the subcommittee that contain material not published in the *Hearings;* (2) fifty interviews in January and March of 1967 with people who participated in making decisions on the TFX program; (3) these journals for the years 1961–1967, containing articles on the TFX — *Aviation Week and Space Technology, Missiles and Rockets* (changed in 1966 to *Technology Week*), *Flight International, Armed Forces Management, Air Force and Space Digest, Space Aeronautics, Astronautics and Aerospace Engineering, Interavia, Fortune,* and *The Saturday Evening Post;* and (4) Hearings before the Senate and House Appropriation Subcommittees on the Department of Defense and before the Senate and House Committees on Armed Services, all of which reviewed the Department of Defense budgets for fiscal years 1964–1968. The other materials listed below were of varying usefulness.

I. *Books*

Danhof, Clarence F. *Government Contracting for Research and Development.* Washington, D.C.: The Brookings Institution, 1966.

Dickinson, Thomas A. *The Aeronautical Dictionary.* New York: Pitman Publishing Corp., 1945.

Hammond, Paul Y. *Organizing for Defense: The American Military Establishment in the Twentieth Century.* Princeton: Princeton University Press, 1961.

Harlan, Neil E. *Management Control in Air Frame Subcontracting.* Boston Division of Research. Harvard Graduate School of Business Administration, 1956.

Hitch, Charles J. *Decision-Making for Defense.* Berkeley and Los Angeles: University of California Press, 1966.

———, and Roland N. McKean. *The Economics of Defense in the Nuclear Age.* Cambridge, Mass.: Harvard University Press, 1960.

Bibliography

Huntington, Samuel P. *Changing Patterns of Military Politics.* New York: The Free Press, 1962.

————. *The Common Defense: Strategic Programs in National Politics.* New York: Columbia University Press, 1961.

————. *The Soldier and the State: The Theory and Politics of Civil-Military Relations.* Cambridge, Mass.: The Belknap Press of Harvard University Press, 1959.

Janowitz, Morris. *The Professional Soldier: A Social and Political Portrait.* New York: The Free Press, 1960.

Kaufmann, William W. *The McNamara Strategy.* New York: Harper and Row, 1964.

Lanz, John E. *Aviation Dictionary.* South Pasadena, Calif.: P. D. and Ione Perkins, 1944.

Little, Arthur D. *How Sick Is the Defense Industry?* Cambridge, Mass., 1963.

Millis, Walter, with Harvey C. Mansfield and Harold Stein. *Arms and the State: Civil-Military Elements in National Policy.* New York: Twentieth Century Fund, 1958.

Mollenhoff, Clark R. *The Pentagon: Politics, Profits and Plunder.* New York: G. P. Putnam's Sons, 1967.

Neustadt, Richard E. *Presidential Power: The Politics of Leadership.* New York: John Wiley and Sons, 1960.

Novick, David (ed.). *Program Budgeting: Program Analysis and the Federal Government.* Cambridge, Mass.: Harvard University Press, 1965.

Peck, Merton J., and Frederic M. Scherer. *The Weapons Acquisition Process: An Economic Analysis.* Boston: Harvard Business School, 1962.

Quade, Edward S. (ed.). *Analysis for Military Decisions.* Chicago: Rand McNally and Co., 1966.

Raymond, Jack. *Power at the Pentagon.* New York: Harper and Row, 1964.

Ries, John C. *The Management of Defense: Organization and Control of United States Armed Forces.* Baltimore: Johns Hopkins University Press, 1964.

Scherer, Frederic M. *The Weapons Acquisition Process: Economic Incentives.* Boston: Harvard Business School, 1964.

Schilling, Warner R., Paul Y. Hammond, and Glenn H. Snyder. *Strategy, Politics and Defense Budgets.* New York: Columbia University Press, 1962.

Simon, Herbert A. *Administrative Behavior: A Study of Decision-Making Processes in Administrative Organizations.* New York: The Macmillan Co., 1961.

Stanford Research Institute. *The Industry-Government Aerospace Relationship.* 2 vols. Menlo Park, Calif., 1963.

Taylor, General Maxwell D. *The Uncertain Trumpet.* New York: Harper and Bros., 1959.

II. *Articles on Research and Development, Weapon System Procurement, and the Department of Defense*

Backe, Bruce. "How Fees May Undermine Incentive Goal," *Aviation Week and Space Technology,* LXXXII (January 11, 1965), 69–72.

Baldwin, Hanson W. "The McNamara Monarchy," *The Saturday Evening Post,* CCXXXVI (March 9, 1963), 8, 11.

Barondes, Lt. Col. Arthur D. "The Congress and R & D," *Air University Review,* XVIII (March–April, 1967), 55–60.

Berg, Lt. Col. Robert S. "Cost-Effectiveness Analysis as an Aid to Weapon System Selection," *Air University Review,* XVII (March–April, 1966), 49–56.

Biedenbender, Richard E., and William G. Ireson. "Incentive Contracts: Genuine Benefits or Hoax?" *Armed Forces Management,* IX (October, 1962), 61–66.

Borklund, C. W. "Lowest Bid Is *Not* Always Lowest Price," *Armed Forces Management,* IX (May, 1963), 40–42.

Breckner, Norman V. "Government Efficiency and the Military 'Buyer-Seller' Device," *Journal of Political Economy,* LXVIII (October, 1960), 469–86.

Brodie, Bernard. "The McNamara Phenomenon," *World Politics,* XVII (July, 1965), 672–87.

Brown, Harold. "Military Aircraft — A Prospectus," *Astronautics and Aeronautics,* II (December, 1964), 40–44.

Brownlow, Cecil. "Standardization Gains Momentum in DOD," *Aviation Week and Space Technology,* LXXXII (March 15, 1965), 69–72.

Bryan, Stanley E. "TFX: A Case in Policy Level Decision-Making," *Academy of Management Journal,* VII (March, 1964), 54–70.

Charles, Robert H. "The So-Called Military-Industrial Complex," *Air Force and Space Digest,* XLVII (October, 1964), 45–47.

Coleman, Col. Jack W., and Major David C. Dellinger. "Incentive

Bibliography

Contracting," *Air University Review,* XVI (November–December, 1964), 31–42.

"Contract Impact on Research to Be Studied," *Aviation Week and Space Technology,* LXXXIV (May 2, 1966), 97.

"Controversial Total Package Plan Tested," *Aviation Week and Space Technology,* LXXXV (Mid-December, 1966), 24–27.

Davita, Sal F. "Selling R & D to the Government," *Harvard Business Review,* XLIII (September–October, 1965), 62–75.

Dawson, Raymond L. "Innovation and Intervention in Defense Policy," in Robert L. Peabody and Nelson W. Polsby (eds.), *New Perspectives on the House of Representatives.* Chicago: Rand McNally and Co., 1963, pp. 273–303.

"Defense Decision Making as McNamara Sees It," *Armed Forces Management,* X (November, 1963), 15–17.

"DOD Plans New Selection Policy," *Aviation Week and Space Technology,* LXXVIII (May 13, 1963), 29.

"DOD Shifts Stir Ire of Congress, Allies," *Aviation Week and Space Technology,* LXXVIII (March 11, 1963), 73–75.

Drake, Hudson B. "Weapon Systems Management: Has the Potential Been Realized?" *Armed Forces Management,* XIII (May, 1967), 66–74.

Enthoven, Alain C. "System Analysis and Decision-Making," *Military Review,* LIII (January, 1963), 7–17.

———, and Harry S. Rowen. "Defense Planning and Organization," in *Public Finances: Needs, Sources, and Utilization* (Princeton: Princeton University Press, 1961), pp. 365–417.

Fink, Donald E. "USAF and DOD Weapons Concepts Outlined at Ordnance Meeting," *Aviation Week and Space Technology,* LXXVII (December 17, 1962), 103ff.

Garvey, Capt. Gerald. "The Changing Management Role of the Military Departments Reconsidered." Parts I and II, *Air University Review,* XV (March–April and May–June, 1964), 38–48 and 35–46.

Getler, Michael. "DOD Emphasis on Concept Stage to Benefit Industry," *Missiles and Rockets,* XVIII (May 23, 1966), 15–16.

———. "Navy to Brief Industry on FDL Ships," *Missiles and Rockets,* XVII (November 22, 1965), 15–16.

"Gilpatric Explains Defense Decision Policy," *Aviation Week and Space Technology,* LXXVIII (February 11, 1963), 32.

Ginsburgh, Col. Robert N., USAF. "The Challenge to Military Professionalism," *Air Force and Space Digest,* XLVII (March, 1964), 50–56.

Gregory, William H. "DOD, NASA Study Common System for Rating Company Performance," *Aviation Week and Space Technology,* LXXVIII (February 4, 1963), 95–99.

Hitch, Charles J. "Economics and Military Operations Research," *Review of Economics and Statistics,* XL (August, 1958), 199–209.

————. "Plans, Programs, and Budgets in the Department of Defense," *Operations Research,* XI (January–February, 1963), 1–17.

"How Defense Intends to Streamline Procurement," *Armed Forces Management,* IX (November, 1962), 78–85.

"How the Budget Decisions Are Reached," *Armed Forces Management,* IX (April, 1963), 13.

Huntington, Samuel P. "Power, Expertise, and the Military Profession," *Daedalus,* XCII (Fall, 1963), 785–808.

"Incentives Prove Useful, But No Cure-All," *Aviation Week and Space Technology,* LXXXI (July 13, 1964), 64.

Kaysen, Carl. "Improving the Efficiency of Military Research and Development," *Public Policy,* XII. Cambridge: Harvard University Graduate School of Public Administration, 1963, pp. 219–273.

Kiker, Douglas. "The Education of Robert McNamara," *Atlantic Monthly,* CCXIX (March, 1967), 49–56.

Klass, Philip J. "DOD May Ease R & D Cost-Sharing Rules," *Aviation Week and Space Technology,* LXXXI (December 28, 1964), 17.

————. "Sweeping Source Selection Changes Sought," *Aviation Week and Space Technology,* LXXXI (October 5, 1964), 24.

Klein, Burton H. "The Decision Making Problem in Development," in *The Rule and Direction of Inventive Activity: Economic and Social Factors.* National Bureau of Economic Research Conference Report. Princeton: Princeton University Press, 1962, pp. 477–508.

Livingston, J. S. "Weapon System Contracting," *Harvard Business Review,* XXXVII (July–August, 1959), 83–92.

MacDonald, Scot. "Evolution of Aircraft Carriers: The Turbulent Post-War Years," *Naval Aviation News* (October, 1963), 22–26.

"The Missile/Space Week: Incentive Contracts Criticized," *Missiles and Rockets,* XVII (November 8, 1965), 10.

Murphy, Charles J. V. "The Desperate Drive to Cut Defense Spending," *Fortune,* LXIX (January, 1964), 95–97, 188–194.

————. "The Education of a Defense Secretary," *Fortune,* LXV (May, 1962), 102–105, 268, 273–74, 278–79.

Bibliography

"Navy Tightens Management, Places Emphasis on Incentive Contracting," *Aviation Week and Space Technology,* LXXXIV (March 21, 1966), 38.

Nelson, Richard. "Uncertainty, Learning and the Economics of Parallel Research and Development Efforts," *Review of Economics and Statistics,* XLIII (November, 1961), 351–64.

"New Controls Planned for R & D," *Armed Forces Management,* VIII (July, 1962), 29–34.

Niblock, Robert W. "Navy to Strengthen Central Authority," *Missiles and Rockets,* XVIII (March 14, 1966), 16.

"Office Overhauls R & D Rules: Tactical Weapons Now Biggest Market," *Missiles and Rockets,* XIV (March 30, 1964), 28–31.

Powell, Craig. "Has the C-5A Procurement Established the Case for TPPC?" *Armed Forces Management,* XII (April, 1966), 73–74.

———. "Have the Services Learned to Live with the Office of Systems Analysis?" *Armed Forces Management,* XII (October, 1965), 73–76.

"Procurement: Changes Begin to Pay Dividends," *Missiles and Rockets,* XII (March 25, 1963), 32–36.

"Research and Engineering: Constant Reviews Yield Sharp Technical Control," *Missiles and Rockets,* XII (March 25, 1963), 41–49.

Roback, Herbert. "Congressional Interest in Weapons Acquisition," *Armed Forces Management,* IX (February, 1963), 40–44.

Schriever, Gen. Bernard A. "The Role of Management in Technological Conflict," *Air University Quarterly Review,* XIV (Winter–Spring, 1962–63), 19–32.

"Secretary of Defense McNamara: 'We Can Afford Whatever Is Necessary,' " *Armed Forces Management,* XII (November, 1965), 35–37.

"Secretary's Authority Reaches Peak," *Missiles and Rockets,* XII (March 25, 1963), 74–75.

Trainor, James. "Project Definition Technique to Be Applied to Many More Programs," *Missiles and Rockets,* XIV (March 9, 1964), 14–15.

Watkins, Harold D. "Improved 'Total Package' Concept Sought," *Aviation Week and Space Technology,* LXXXIV (May 2, 1966), 95–99.

"What Tying Dollars to Military Decisions Means to Defense Management," *Armed Forces Management,* IX (November, 1962), 86–91.

"Why R & D Continues to Influence National Policy," *Armed Forces Management,* IX (November, 1962), 59–65.

Wilson, George C. "Services Draft Source Selection Guides," *Aviation Week and Space Technology,* LXXXII (May 17, 1965), 88–89.

Yarmolinsky, Adam. "How the Pentagon Works," *Atlantic Monthly,* CCXIX (March, 1967), 56–62.

Zuckert, Eugene M. "The Service Secretary: Has He a Useful Role?" *Foreign Affairs,* XLIV (April, 1966), 458–79.

"Zuckert Gives Views of Aerospace Issues: Interview with Secretary of the Air Force Eugene M. Zuckert," *Aviation Week and Space Technology,* LXXX (March 2, 1964), 72–73.

III. *United States Government Publications*

A. Congress

House of Representatives. Committee on Armed Services. *Hearings before Subcommittee No. 2 on the Department of Defense Decision to Reduce the Number and Types of Manned Bombers in the Strategic Air Command.* 89th Cong., 2nd Sess., 1966.

House of Representatives. Committee on Armed Services. *Report of Subcommittee No. 2 on the Department of Defense Decision to Reduce the Number and Types of Manned Bombers in the Strategic Air Command.* 89th Cong., 2nd Sess., April 4, 1966.

House of Representatives. Subcommittee of the Committee on Government Operations. *Hearings on Systems Development and Management.* 5 vols. 87th Cong., 2nd Sess., 1962.

Joint Committee on Atomic Energy. *Hearings on Nuclear Propulsion for Naval Surface Vessels.* 88th Cong., 1st Sess., 1963.

B. Executive Branch

U.S. Bureau of the Budget. *Report to the President on Government Contracting for Research and Development,* April 30, 1962. Annex 1.

Secretary of the Air Force, Office of Information, Internal Information Division. "United States Air Force Fact Sheet on the F-111A," July, 1966.

Air Force Manual 70-10. *System Source Selection Board Procedures 18 January 1963.*

Air Force Regulation No. 70-15. *Proposal Evaluation and Source Selection Procedures 20 September 1965.*

Air Force Regulation No. 70-15. *System Source Selection Procedures 24 April 1962.*

Bibliography

Air Force Regulation 80-3. System Source Selection Board, Wright-Patterson Air Force Base, Ohio. *Instructions to the Chairman of Evaluation Group for System 324A (TFX/F-111)*. Exhibit 80 of the 1963 *TFX Hearings*. Files of the Permanent Investigating Subcommittee of the Committee on Government Operations, U.S. Senate.

Department of the Air Force. *System Source Selection: A Descriptive Booklet* (undated), Exhibit No. 44 of the 1963 *TFX Hearings* in the Files of the Permanent Investigating Subcommittee of the Committee on Government Operations, U.S. Senate.

Department of Defense. *Armed Services Procurement Regulations.*

Department of Defense. *The Changing Patterns of Defense Procurement*. Washington, D.C.: Government Printing Office, 1962.

Office of the Secretary of Defense. *Department of Defense Guide to the Evaluation of the Performance of Major Development Contractors*. Washington, D.C.: Government Printing Office, 1964.

Department of Defense. *Five Year Trends in Defense Procurement, FY 1958-FY 1962*. Washington, D.C.: Government Printing Office, 1963.

Department of Defense. *Incentive Contracting Guide Prepared by the Office of Assistant Secretary of Defense for Installations and Logistics*. Washington, D.C.: Government Printing Office, 1963.

Department of Defense Directive No. 3200.9. *Initiation of Engineering and Operational Systems Development*. 1 July 1965.

Department of Defense. *Maximum Improvement in Air Weapon Systems in Minimum Time: Summary of Actions Taken to Reduce the Time Required for Research, Development, Procurement, and Production of Manned Aircraft Weapon Systems*. (Report of the Robertson Committee). Washington, D.C.: Government Printing Office, February 8, 1957.

Office of the Secretary of Defense. *Methods of Estimating Fixed-Wing Airframe Costs*. Vol. I (Revised), PRC R-547A. Prepared for the Office of the Secretary of Defense under Contract by the Planning Research Corporation. Los Angeles, 1967.

Department of Defense. *Procurement Presentation to the Procurement Subcommittee of the Committee on Armed Services, U.S. Senate*. Washington, D.C.: Government Printing Office, 1960.

Department of Defense. Office of the Secretary of Defense. *Programming System for the Office of the Secretary of Defense, 25 June 1962*. Washington, D.C.: Government Printing Office, 1963.

C. The RAND Corporation

Asher, Harold. *Cost-Quantity Relationships in the Airframe Industry.* RAND Report R-291. Santa Monica: RAND Corp., 1956.

Barro, Stephen M. *Some Methodological Problems of Airframe Cost Estimation.* RAND Paper 3305. Santa Monica: RAND Corp., 1966.

Downs, Anthony. *A Theory of Bureaucracy.* RAND Paper 3031. Santa Monica: RAND Corp., 1964.

Fisher, G. H. *The World of Program Budgeting.* RAND Paper 3361. Santa Monica: RAND Corp., 1966.

Glennan, Thomas K. *Innovation and Product Quality Under the Total Package Procurement Concept.* RAND Memorandum 5097-PR. Santa Monica: RAND Corp., 1966.

————. *Methodological Problems in Evaluating the Effectiveness of Military Aircraft Development,* RAND Paper 3357. Santa Monica: RAND Corp., 1966.

Kermisch, J. J., and A. J. Tenzer. *On the Role of the Cost Analyst in a Weapon System Study.* RAND Paper 3360. Santa Monica: RAND Corp., 1966.

Klein, Burton A., William H. Mecklin, and E. G. Mesthene. *Military Research and Development Policies.* RAND Report 333. Santa Monica: RAND Corp., 1958.

Margolis, M. A. *Use of Cost-Estimating Relationships in the Airframe Industry.* RAND Paper 3472. Santa Monica: RAND Corp., 1966.

Marschak, T. A. *The Role of Project Histories in the Study of R & D.* RAND Paper 2850. Santa Monica: RAND Corp., 1965.

Marshall, A. W., and W. H. Meckling. *Predictability of Costs, Time, and Success of Development.* RAND Paper 1821. Santa Monica: RAND Corp., 1960.

Novick, David. *Costing Tomorrow's Weapon Systems.* RAND Report RM-3170-PR. Santa Monica: RAND Corp., 1962.

————. *Identifying R & D: A Management Problem.* RAND Paper 2135. Santa Monica: RAND Corp., 1960.

————. *Origin and History of Program Budgeting.* RAND Paper 3427. Santa Monica: RAND Corp., 1966.

————. *Separating Research from Research and Development.* RAND Paper 2907. Santa Monica: RAND Corp., 1964.

————. *System and Total Force Cost Analysis.* RAND Report RM-2695-PR. Santa Monica: RAND Corp., 1961.

————. *Weapon-System Cost Methodology.* RAND Report 287. Santa Monica: RAND Corp., 1956.

Bibliography

Perry, Robert L. *The Mythography of Military R & D*. RAND Paper 3356. Santa Monica: RAND Corp., 1966.
————. *Variable Sweep: A Case History of Multiple Re-Innovation*. RAND Paper 3459. Santa Monica: RAND Corp., 1966.
Quade, E. S. *Cost-Effectiveness: An Introduction and Overview*. RAND Paper 3134. Santa Monica: RAND Corp., 1965.
Schlesinger, James R. *Analysis and Defense in the Sixties*. RAND Paper 3050. Santa Monica: RAND Corp., 1965.
————. *On Relating Non-Technical Elements to System Studies*. RAND Paper 3545. Santa Monica: RAND Corp., 1967.

IV. *Unpublished Material, Speeches, Case Studies, Newspapers, and British Documents*

Advanced Management Associates, Inc. "The C-5A: The Anatomy of a Procurement." Three Case Studies, 1965.
Alexander, Marvin M., Jr. (Manager, Structural Sciences, Fort Worth Division of the General Dynamics Corporation). "Structural Problems Associated with Variable Geometry" (undated).
Aviation Daily.
Barron's National Business & Financial Weekly.
Beckler, Bernard Saul. "The Pricing Process in Defense Procurement." Unpublished Ph.D dissertation, American University, 1963–64.
Charles, Robert H. (Assistant Secretary of the Air Force for Installation and Logistics). "The Total Package Procurement Concept," Address before the Defense Industry Advisory Council, February 18, 1966.
Dudas, Dan L. "The F-111: A New Dimension in Fighter-Bombers" (undated).
"The F-111." A Brochure Prepared by the General Dynamics Corporation, December, 1966.
"The F-111 Newsletter: A Report Issued Periodically by General Dynamics on Activities in the F-111 Variable-Wing Aircraft Program," Nos. 1–5 (undated).
Fox, J. Ronald. "The Control of Schedules and Costs in Major Weapon and Space Programs." The American Society of Military Comptrollers, 1963.
Great Britain. *Statement on the Defense Estimates for 1965*. Presented to Parliament by the Secretary of State for Defense, February, 1965. London: HMSO (Her Majesty's Stationery Office).

194

————. *Statement on the Defense Estimates for 1966. Part I. The Defense Review; Part II, The Defense Estimates for 1966–67.* London: HMSO.

————. *Statement on the Defense Estimates for 1967.* Presented to Parliament by the Secretary of State for Defense, February, 1967. London: HMSO.

————. *The Defense Estimates for 1967–68 for the Year Ending 31 March 1968.* London: HMSO.

Howard, David C. "Weapons Systems: Costs and Contract Values." Air War College Associate Programs (undated).

McNamee, John. "A Summary of Major Innovations in the Weapon Systems Acquisition Process." A paper made available by Douglas Aircraft Co., Inc., to the Harvard Business School for use in the Defense Marketing and Project Management Course, 1965.

The New York Times.

Prahl, Val. (Manager, Flight Test Department, Fort Worth Division of General Dynamics). "Flight Test Report — F-111." Presentation at the Society of Experimental Test Pilots Symposium at the Beverly Hilton, Beverly Hills, California, September 24, 1965.

Russell, John R. (Director of Systems Analysis and Chief Consultant, Incentive Contracting, Harbridge House, Inc.). "Effects of Incentive Contracting." Address before the Washington, D.C., Chapter of the National Contract Management Association, March 16, 1966.

TFX Case (A). Prepared by Mr. Dan Dudas at the Harvard Graduate School of Business Administration, 1964.

TFX Case Studies A-D. Prepared under the direction of Mr. J. Ronald Fox, Harvard Graduate School of Business Administration, 1966.

Waks, Norman. "Selective Competition in New Air Weapon Procurement." Unpublished Ph.D. dissertation, Harvard Graduate School of Business Administration, 1961.

Wall Street Journal.

Washington Post.

INDEX